CW00431148

ANGELA COUSINS

KIDS FROM OVER THE *Water*

An Edwardian working-class childhood in south-east London

The annotated memoirs of Keturah Daveney (1895–1982)

ANGELA COUSINS

KIDS FROM OVER THE
Water

An Edwardian working-class
childhood in south-east London

The annotated memoirs of Keturah Daveney (1895–1982)

MEREO
Cirencester

Published by Mereo

1A The Market Place Cirencester Gloucestershire GL7 2PR
info@memoirsbooks.co.uk | www.memoirspublishing.com

Kids from over the water

All Rights Reserved.
Copyright (main text) ©Angela Cousins

Extracts from An Edwardian
Working-Class Childhood ©Thompson Daveney

No part of this book may be reproduced or transmitted in any form or
by any means, graphic, electronic, or mechanical, including
photocopying, recording, taping or by any information storage or
retrieval system, without the permission in writing from the copyright
holder. The right of Angela Cousins to be identified as the author of
this work has been asserted in accordance with the Copyright,
Designs and Patents Act 1988 sections 77 and 78.

Despite considerable searching, it has not been possible to identify the
copyright holders of every photograph. The author will be pleased to
pay an appropriate fee if contacted via the publisher.

The views expressed in this work are solely those of the author and do
not necessarily reflect the views of the publisher, and the publisher
hereby disclaims any responsibility for them.

ISBN: 978-1-86151-163-8

I dedicate this book to the fond memory of my aunt, Keturah Daveney, and her brother, my father, Walter Filmer.

Contents

Foreword

Foreword

In 1977, her eighty-second year, my aunt Keturah Daveney began writing about her early life in Walworth in south-east London, where she had lived from 1900, when she was five years old, until her marriage. Keturah had been much saddened by the death of her beloved husband Will, so, encouraged by her family, she began to write all she could remember about her young life.

Writing became her therapy, and her finished work was turned into a small book entitled *An Edwardian Working Class Childhood*. A few copies were produced for family members, but although her children subsequently suggested that her work could be published, she was not interested and would not consider the idea of even minor editorial changes.

I treasure my own copy and have read it many times, always delighting in Keturah's quirky stories, sometimes being moved to tears by the dogged determination of her family to maintain their dignity and cope as best they could against the odds. However, as I came closer to the age of my aunt at the time she was writing, I began to recognise that this little book is a rather important historical document. It is not unique in one sense, in that stories similar to hers could be retold across the country many thousands of times, but it is remarkable in that this is her personal story, full of detailed memories of a family's effort to hold their heads high despite challenging circumstances.

Last year I approached Keturah's two surviving children about the possibility of writing a book based on their mother's own work, and was delighted when they expressed their warm approval of the idea. I could not have written *Kids From Over The Water* without their blessing and am grateful to them for entrusting me with the job of faithfully interpreting her writing.

Thanks are therefore due to my cousins, Beryl Gurney and Thompson Daveney, for permitting me to edit and develop Keturah's original script, and also to my sister Rosemary Moore, who has shown much interest in this book and proof-read the first draft. The staff at Southwark Local History Library have been most helpful and my tolerant husband, Lionel Cousins, has given invaluable encouragement and support.

Keturah did not write chronologically and there were few paragraphs to give structure to the text, so to aid comprehension it has been necessary to edit and adapt some of her writing and arrange it into chapters. Additional comment has been added as appropriate. What has been of the greatest importance to me has been to capture Keturah's style and spirit so that her words and emotions would continue to communicate to the reader across the years. I hope that I have done her justice.

ACC
West Hanney, Oxfordshire, 2013

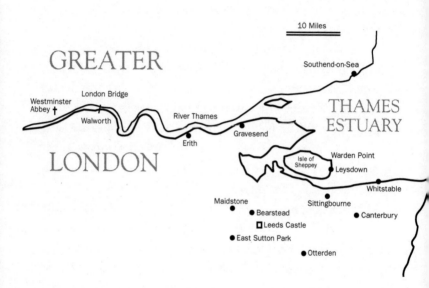

Map of significant locations in Keturah Filmer's story

Keturah Filmer's family - 1900

The surname 'Filmer' appears in documents from the mid thirteenth century onwards. Several branches of the family were initially concentrated in an area of Kent south of Sittingbourne and between Maidstone and Canterbury. A family historian believes that the original name may have been 'Fynmer'. Filmer remains a fairly common name in the south of England to the present time and Filmers have also emigrated round the world, in particular to Canada, Australia and South Africa.

John Apps Budds Filmer, Keturah's father, was born in 1859 in the village of Bearstead, near Maidstone in Kent. He was the youngest of seven children, having four brothers and two sisters, George, Walter, Jasper, Alfred, Ann and Jane. Two of his brothers emigrated to Canada and many of their descendants still live in British Columbia. In 1885 John married Charlotte Ellen Hall and between then and 1907 Charlotte became pregnant thirteen times, eight children surviving into adulthood.

I was my mother's sixth child. The oldest of the family, whose name was Harry, was ten years older than me.

Annie was the second child, Clara the third, Margaret the fourth, Jack the fifth, and me, Keturah[1], the sixth. Then came Noel, Tom, Jean, Jimmy (who died) and Walter. My mother had three other children but they died in her early married life.

Keturah's family moved from Bearstead to Walworth, a densely-populated area of south-east London, in 1900, because there was no work for John in his village. At that time there were eight children living at home; Harry was fifteen and had just begun a seven-year printing apprenticeship. The three older girls would later leave home when they left school at fourteen, all working either in private service or as chambermaids in London hotels. Younger family members were Jack aged seven, Keturah five, Noel three and Tom, a baby; subsequently three more children were born, Jean, Jimmy and lastly my father, Walter. Jimmy's all too brief life will be described later on.

John's father, also John, was a journeyman bricklayer who moved from Bearstead to Newington in south-east London after the death of his wife Jane, when young John was about three years old. Young John ran away from home when he was a teenager, as his stepmother, Eliza, was cruel to him. He served before the mast in sailing ships of the British, American and Chilean navies before jumping ship in America and riding the railroads to Canada to visit his brothers. John returned to England in the early 1880s, sporting a large American eagle tattooed on his back! He married Charlotte Hall in 1885.

1. Keturah – An Old Testament name. Keturah was one of Abraham's wives, (Genesis 25 1-4) and bore him many sons. The first Keturah in this branch of the Filmer family was Keturah Apps, born c. 1760. The name continues through the generations until the present day.

After John and Charlotte were married, John's aunt Keturah set them up in a small shop in south London, where their first child Harry was born. The shop failed, but by 1891 John had obviously decided to make use of his mast-climbing skills, as the census return indicates that by then he had become a scaffolder. John was paid by the day, his work being dependent on availability and of course, the weather; he was never work-shy, but was often out of work through no fault of his own.

Throughout Keturah's story her father comes over as a tough, hard-working, responsible man, of whom she was very fond.

Dear old Dad, he was a tower of strength to us all, for this small man had travelled round the world on a windjammer, and he could climb up the highest building to put up scaffolding, ignoring the steep drop below. I have seen him with two sacks of cement, one under each arm, going up the buildings. He never knew fear. He eventually became a 'ganger' in charge of the men who erected the scaffold, and he examined every pole the men put up. If he saw a bad knot he made the men undo it, and if the men did it again he would sack the one who hadn't heeded his warning. He used to say men's lives depended on the scaffold.

I remember him joining the 'Builders' Union' and sending me to a pub in Blackfriars to pay his threepence subs. He had a white union card with pink stripes down the middle; the man who marked my father's card said to me "It's all for your benefit my little girl, for when you grow up". Funny isn't it? The man had a handkerchief round his neck; today they wear a collar and tie.

Charlotte Hall grew up in Camberwell and her father was a stereotyper[2], a highly skilled job in the printing trade. He was a departmental manager at Harrison and Son, the world-famous stamp printers, in the West End of London. Apparently he designed the laurel leaves on postage stamps and also invented the glue that really did stick the stamps onto the envelopes!

Charlotte was one of nine children and in 1881 was recorded in the census as 'a servant in laundry'. From Keturah's descriptions she was a hard-working, gentle but resilient woman who accepted her lot and did her best to be a good wife, mother and neighbour.

My wonderful mother knew a lot about nursing and I have known her and myself sit up all night putting linseed poultices on a patient's chest, and spoon-feed them with weak tea and brandy, (which she bought herself for threepence, sometimes that would have been all the money she had). She used to say "I'll earn some tomorrow". My mother said that the poultices made the patient exhausted and the brandy-water helped them; believe me, it seemed that if my mother was nursing them they seemed to get better. Our doctor used to say "If Mrs Filmer is there I cannot do more".

2. By the 19th century, type could be cast and set into text in a single operation, but the soft metal casts tended to wear down quickly in the printing process, and had to be replaced with fresh type. Stereotyping began by making a mould of set type using a heat-resistant papier-mache. Molten metal was then poured into the mould to create the cast plate, which was then used in the printing process.

CHAPTER TWO

The family at home

The house in Townley Street, Walworth; paying the rent - Aunt Annie to the rescue; a stitch in time; list slippers; DIY

When I was five years old my father and mother had to move from a lovely cottage opposite Bearstead Green, where I was born, because my father needed to find work. We moved to a small terraced house in a South London back street where there were no trees or fields. It was a dull and uninteresting street, just rows of small houses.

Initially, the 1901 census indicates, the family lived in Albert House, one of a group of large tenement buildings in Walworth. However Keturah starts her story when they have moved on to their permanent home in nearby Townley Street, adjacent to East Street, famous for its street market both then and now[3]. Less than a mile away was London Bridge and the River Thames, while nearby was the Elephant and Castle.

Compared to the freedom of Bearstead Green, the crowded, dirty back streets would have been a poor

3. East Street Market – one of London's oldest, largest and busiest markets. Known locally as 'the lane', there has been a market on this site since the sixteenth century. Nowadays the market is particularly known for West Indian and African food, material and household goods.

substitute for the children as a place to play. Keturah gives detailed descriptions not only of the house, which would be her home for many years to come, but of the basic, primitive standards of living with which they had to contend. The house was rented, and in future pages there will be other references to the struggle to pay the weekly rent, but now it's time for Keturah to open the front door off the street.

In our house there were four rooms and a scullery which had a stone floor. There was also a stone copper and a stone sink over which there was a small window which overlooked a yard where we had a shed. Our lavatory was opposite the scullery window so that if you forgot to lock the door you could see the person who was sitting on the lavatory. The lavatory was a long concrete slab over which was a wooden plank with a hole made for sitting on. There were no decent bedrooms or a bathroom, well there was always the public baths where my elder brothers and sisters went. We at home, us younger ones, had to bath in a large tin bath in front of the fire. One summer my dad made a contraption; he put a hose pipe on the tap in the scullery and made a hole through the scullery wall for the hose to go through and then he made the contraption. Beforehand he made a wooden rack for us to walk on over the concrete ground in the yard. My mother made us wear mackintosh pants that she had made out of an old mac, then, one by one, while my father squirted the hose pipe, we ran through the water and mother was at the other side to catch us with a bath towel. My dad said it would make us strong. Ha, yes!!

At the back of our yard there was a piece of waste ground where the street traders[4] kept their barrows and carts. The ponies and donkeys were stabled in little sheds in the back yards of these homes to which the only means of access was through the front door. I used to laugh when I saw ponies coming out of a house with a clothes line full of washing hanging over their heads.

Throughout Keturah's writings there are many references to the never-ending problem of ensuring that there was enough money to pay the landlady at the end of the week. John earned money when work was available and could never rely on a daily wage, but there was always an assumption that Charlotte would manage whatever money was in her purse and would ensure that the family did not go without food or coal and that the rent would be paid. When she was well enough, Charlotte worked long hours in the local laundry, but there were many hungry mouths to feed and sometimes the struggle was almost too much and extreme measures had to be taken.

Once again my father was out of work, but this was nothing unusual. Times were hard, damned hard too. Not a penny unless you worked for it, and often there wasn't any work to do. You could either starve or go into the workhouse. Somehow my mother managed to keep the "ship afloat" working at the ironing board, slaving at the laundry. My dad had been out of a job for weeks this time,

4. The street traders were commonly known as costermongers.

the weather had been awful, snow and ice, and there was little outside building work. But this time my mother had got behind with the rent. Our landlady was a godly soul and had often said "Never mind Mrs Filmer, you can pay sixpence [2.4p] off the arrears; it's not your fault that they neglect the poor people, you work very hard and your husband still can't find any work I presume."

On this particular Monday I was away from school with a bad cough, so when the land lady called for the rent I handed her the rent book, together with the eight shillings and sixpence [42p] for the arrears. She then said "Tell your mother that I have sold this house to a very kind gentleman who will look after your mother in the fashion I have. He will be calling next Monday." I told my mother the news when she came home from the laundry and she said she was sorry.

The new landlord came about the same time as our landlady and I handed him the rent book together with the eight shillings and sixpence arrears. He looked very hard at me, opened the book then handed it back to me saying He looked at it and said: "I see your mother owes seven pounds arrears." "Yes" I answered, "our landlady lets my mother pay six pence a week off the arrears, because she's sorry for my mother and my dad has been out of work a long time this winter." "Does your father know your mother owes rent?" he asked. "Oh no", I replied, "He must never know." "Well...", said the landlord, but before he could say what he was going to say, I interrupted "My dad expects the house to be run as usual, in or out of work, and he would be cross with my mother, he detests debt." "I cannot accept the sixpence off the arrears, whatever your circumstances, so when I call next week I want all the arrears in full, do you understand?" "Yes" I replied, "I fully understand."

All the next week my mother worked overtime at the laundry to make up the arrears, and my sisters helped a little, but all my mother could raise was half the arrears which was three pounds and ten shillings [£1.50] and the eight shillings rent. [40p] On the next Monday I stayed away from school because my cough was still troublesome, so when the landlord called, I handed him the rent book together with the eight shillings rent and the three pounds ten shillings, and I also gave him my mother's message that she would pay the rest next Monday without fail.

The landlord made no answer but only took the eight shillings rent and handed me back the rent book. Then he called "Bill, Jim", and up came a van and two men jumped out. The landlord said "Go in and see what they've got", and the two men walked into our house, pushed by me and went into our parlour. The men shouted, "Gov', they've got a Chippendale suite, a Victorian couch, a round table with a lamp on it, a mirror on the wall. Shall we pull the mirror off the wall? And they've got a piano". The landlord said "Bring out the piano and don't touch anything else".

I saw the van drive away with our piano and sadly watched it through my tears until it was out of sight. I closed the door and walked back into the parlour and stood where our piano had stood. To think that my mother had bought our piano earlier in her marriage at a time when her family wasn't so large and debt was unknown. I walked into

9

our kitchen and sat on the stool by the fire, trying to find a way out – I really could not think that such people as our landlord existed.

A knock on the street door interrupted my thoughts and there stood Mr Tomkins, the Missionary, holding a small bunch of flowers. "Give these to your dear mother, and you read the text." I said "Let us read the text together Mr Tomkins." And as we read I could not hide my tears, so then I told him our sad news, I knew my secret would be safe with him, he would never tell anyone. Mr Tomkins said how sorry he was, "Such a lady is your mother. Please tell her she can have the loan of my organ until I come back from Africa, I'm going tomorrow." I thanked Mr Tomkins, closed the street door and went into the parlour and wondered what the organ would look like where our piano had stood.

I must, I thought, start preparing the children's dinner, but that was a while away yet. Another knock on the street door, but that was only the "cats' meat man". Only a miracle could get my mother out of this one, my dad must not know; perhaps he was lacking in common sense, but he was a good dad. Still wondering. Another knock on the door

"Aunt Annie", I exclaimed, "what are you doing here?" Aunt Annie was my father's youngest sister, she had never married. "Well" she said, "I have a very bad cough and have three days off work." (She had worked in London hotels for years). "So have I Aunt", I said as I made a large pot of tea – I thought she'd need more than one cup after what I had to tell her. When I had told all Aunt Annie said "Oh my goodness, your father must never know. It's a good thing they didn't take the furniture, that could never be replaced, it's an heirloom from our grandfather, left to your father to be passed on to you children later on. Whatever can be done?" "There is one thing we can do Aunt" I said, "buy another piano." "How?" she asked. "On easy terms" I said, "I have the three pounds ten shillings that the landlord wouldn't take. You come with me and sign until mother can go." "Where?" she asked. "To Hicks in the New Kent Road, they know me and Mum because they used to tune our piano, and Mr Hicks belongs to Harry's club." "But don't you think we should wait and tell your mother?" said Aunt. "No", I answered, "let's go now, Mum always trusts me, come on Aunt, we can be back before the children come home."

In no time at all we were in Mr Hicks' piano shop. I stood aside while Aunt Annie was talking and I saw Mr Hicks shake his head. This didn't seem very helpful, but I wasn't near enough to hear what he was saying, then I saw Aunt Annie open her handbag and show something to Mr Hicks, it was her Post Office Savings Book. They both went into the office, so I was at a complete loss as to what was taking place, so while I waited I tinkled on an open piano. When they came out of the office Mr Hicks opened the door and shook hands with Aunt Annie and smiled at me. Aunt Annie said nothing to me as we went on until she passed the pastry cook shop. "Go in and buy eight meat pies, they'll do for our dinners". Still she didn't say a word until we arrived home and then she bust out laughing. I couldn't restrain myself any longer. "Aunt, do tell me what Mr Hicks said to you." "Well" she said, "I have bought your mother a piano, money down. I am not without money you know, and besides, your mother has been very good to me, she gave me a home when I had nowhere to go, nursed me when I was ill and said that her home was my home, so I am pleased to be able to give her this new piano". I threw my arms about her neck and said "Aunt, I'll always look after you, when you are old you can live with me until the end". I kept my promise and she really did live with me until she died.

The new piano came that very same afternoon, and no one, apart from Aunt Annie, Mum and I, ever knew. The only remark my dad made was "Kit, you must have given the piano a good polish up", so I answered "Yes, I have given it its Christmas polish up". Never another word.

Times were often hard and during one bad winter my dad was out of work for six weeks. One day he met a man who used to play old songs on a street barrel organ. He asked my dad if he could sing, and would he come out with him and sing. My dad said he would go with him, anything to earn money. Well this man used to have a monkey sitting on top of the organ and as my dad started to sing in his powerful voice "Kathleen Mavauneen", the monkey jumped on him and tore his coat. As my dad tried to beat him off, the monkey went for the seat of his trousers and tore the seat nearly to pieces. Luckily my dad wasn't hurt, but he had a very embarrassing walk home. My mother said "That's the only pair of trousers you have got and the seat is torn to ribbons. Now what are we going to do?" Just at that precise moment the postman dropped a card through the letter box and I handed it to my dad. "Good Lord" he said, "it's from a firm of builders and they have offered me a job and I can start tomorrow, that's good isn't it?" He was elated. My mother said very quietly "But you haven't got any trousers, these you have are beyond repair, whatever can we do?"

I then had an idea, "I know", I said, "I will try to borrow a pair from my friend's father." I then went and collected three pairs from my friend's house and my dad tried them all on but not one of the pairs fitted him, so we were all down in the dumps again. My mother then said "Can't we make a pair out of that old brown coat, the one in the cupboard that my brother Jim gave you, and you said "I don't want your brother's left off". I might add that my mother's brother Jim was over six feet tall and my dad five foot one inch tall. However out came the coat and my mother looked at it; my dad, being a sailor who had twice sailed round the world, knew about sewing sails. "Yes" he said, "let's have a go." "We'll do it, even if we have to sit up all night," I promised him.

My mother did the cuttings and pinnings, but when it came to the sewing part we didn't have any brown cotton, only blue or white, so down in the dumps we went. "Just a minute" I said, "I'll run up to the Jews", (a little shop at one corner of our street),[5] "I'll ask them to trust us with a reel of brown cotton until Friday." My mother looked at the clock and said "They'll be shut by now", but I dashed out and was just in time. "Mrs Hymans, could you trust us with a reel of brown cotton until Friday, only my dad has torn his trousers so he won't be able to go to work tomorrow"? She looked at me and said "You would get away with anything", as she handed me the brown cotton. Now we

5. In the early 1900s there was a sizeable community of Jewish stallholders and shopkeepers in the Walworth area. The 'Borough Synagogue' had opened in 1867 and attached to this was a Jewish School.

were all shoulders to the wheel, cutting, joining, sewing, and by three o'clock in the morning, just three hours before my dad was due to leave for work, the brown trousers were finished, with joins nearly all over them. Now only the pressing to do. My mother was too tired, so I pressed them; what an achievement to see those brown trousers hanging over the chair-back, all ready for my dad to start work.

Exactly at 5.30 my dad went to work. He had to walk all the way to the City as he didn't have any money for his bus fare. I can see him now with his brown trousers on, putting his big hammer in the back of his thick leather belt. The weather had improved, the ice was thawing, but later it poured with rain, and in a little while my dad returned soaked to the skin, right up past his knees. My mother put the brown trousers on the fireguard to dry and soon they were steaming. "Well Jack" my mother said, "I do not know what we are going to do for money because there's not a penny in the house, and I am not well enough to go to the laundry. I thought you would ask for a sub today". I spoke up quickly, "I'll go to Harriet's mother, she'll lend us some money." I looked over to my dad, (he hated the thought of borrowing), and he was holding out his hand with a half a crown [12p] in it. "Goodness", I said, "our troubles are over". "Did you think I would come home without asking for a sub? In fact, I didn't have to ask the boss, when he knew how many children I had, he offered me a sub, in fact he made me a 'ganger', so the old brown coat brought luck after all".

My mother said we must pray for fine weather, but my dad said "Won't matter about wet or fine weather now as I've got plenty of inside work, and what's more, I can find

14

enough work for twenty men to last for eighteen months".
I put my fingers to my ears, I could hardly believe the
wonderful news, it was so exciting, at last I could show off
with all the new dresses I could have. When I went to bed
that night I prayed to God, "Thank you God, I have so
much to thank you for on this particular day".

Keturah writes in some detail about 'list slippers[6]':

I often had to go to school in what we called "list slippers".
Now these were made by a neighbour who sold them for
threepence [1.2p] a pair. They were made of different
coloured striped pieces of felt woven on a last into little
squares. If the weather was good and dry they were not
too bad, but woe betide if it rained, they were like sinking
boats. I always remember walking into my classroom in
school after it had been raining, they left pattern marks all
over the floor, and if I happened to have a seat near the
fire, they would steam up, and it wasn't a very pleasant
experience. I leave it to the readers who I do hope will read
this, to imagine how uncomfortable it was, but in our
position, and despite all the difficulties, we were not
unhappy. We were indeed happy children, moreover we
never missed the comforts of today because we never had
them, but when you saw children slurping along in boots
miles too big for them, and many thinly-clad, it still makes
me feel sad.

★ ★ ★

6. List slippers were made of a woven material, including the soles. They were often worn when quiet
was needed, ie in a sick room. They were also worn in the navy by gunners and mates when a ship
went into action – anyone entering the room where gunpowder was stored wore list slippers to avoid
striking a spark from spilled gunpowder on the floor.

One Sunday we were sitting down to begin our dinner when one of the legs on my chair broke and I fell on the floor. My brothers and Jean laughed, thinking it was a huge joke, but when I showed them the cut on my leg and asked them if that was something to laugh about, they said they were sorry, and my mum and dad were sorry too. My dad said "This will never happen again because I will make you all a chair each". The next Saturday saw us all off with my dad to the wood yard to buy the wood for our new chairs. "Come on, seeing as you are all going to have a chair you must all help carry the wood home".

For the next two months we were all busy helping my dad with the making of the chairs. Jack's duty was to hold the wood while dad planed it, Tom had to hand up the nails to Dad, Noel's duty was to measure the chairs with my dad's big rule and then measure our height, but every time he measured us he declared we had grown half an inch. "It has to be one thing or another, either your rule is wrong, or the family must have their shoes on at one time and not at the other time!"

My job was to sweep up the sawdust from the floor. Jean said she would be glad when Dad didn't have to bang the hammer so hard because it made her jump, and Mother murmured quietly, "so much confusion".

At long last the chairs were finished and Dad put the five chairs behind the back of the table, this was a six foot wooden table that he had made two years beforehand. My dad was delighted with the chairs. "Ha", he said, "they are a set, they match the table, they're finished" he exclaimed with a broad grin. Noel looked at the chairs, "There's one thing you've forgotten Dad, seeing they are all alike, how will we know whose chair we are sitting on, except Jack, his chair is bigger than ours?" "But you'll all be bigger soon, so what's the difference?" said Dad. "I was thinking of now", said Noel, "not when we are bigger". "Well Noel", asked Dad, "have you any suggestions?" "Yes I have" he said, "I will paint their Christian names on each chair". "What a splendid idea Noel" my mother said. "I'll start straight away, beginning with the eldest, that's Jack, and working downwards". So Noel, with his air of confidence, started to paint the names. My name came next and I could see that he was hesitating, and for some reason known only to himself, he missed my name out and went on with the others until he had finished, all but mine. Then he went over to Dad and whispered something in his ear, but unfortunately Dad was deaf in that ear, so at last he went to my mother, and she spelt it out very loudly, KETURAH. Noel went to my chair and painted my name, but when he turned it round it read like this, HARUTEK; "Splendid" he said, "I have painted your name backwards so no one will be able to pronounce it". My dad said "That wasn't a nice thing to have done", and Mother agreed. "Oh sorry, it's the devil in me" said Noel "I'll repaint it Kit". "Oh please don't, Noel" I like it, I really like it that way".

A few years later my dad found a permanent job so my mother need not go out to work any more. This was good news indeed, especially when we were able to move to a larger house with three bedrooms. When Dad bought a new dining room suite the wooden chairs were put away under the stairs for us to have when we were married.

CHAPTER THREE

Putting food on the table

East Street Market; The sad tale of Joey; school dinner tickets; 'Otts 'addick; hungry school children and a petty thief; workhouse food; the Robert Browning Turkey and Pudding Club

Keturah never uses the word 'hunger', although she makes it clear that there were days when there was only just enough food to go round. It goes without saying that Charlotte must have been an exceptionally competent manager as well as a good cook; with little money and no refrigeration, it would have been a constant challenge to feed her brood. Most of the daily shopping would have been done at the shops and stalls of East Street market, which was just round the corner, and Keturah gives a wonderful illustration of just how far she could make a few pennies go when it was her turn to go shopping.

> I would like you to come shopping with me in our street market. Imagine my mum giving me a two shilling piece

[10p], enough to buy food for seven people. My first purchase would have been at the grocer's shop where I bought two ounces [about 60 gms] of tea at a shilling a pound; I got it at that price because it contained a little tea dust. I then proceeded to another grocer's shop because their sugar was a little cheaper; one pound, or sixteen ounces [450 gms] of sugar at two pence a pound. Then on to the provision shop for two ounces of fresh butter at one shilling a pound and two ounces of margarine at eight pence a pound. Next on to a stall where I bought an English wild rabbit for ten pence or a shilling, I paid ten pence. Now to the butchers where I bought one pennyworth of English pork trimmings. At the greengrocers stall I bought pounds of potatoes for two pence and one pound of pot herbs for a penny-halfpenny. All this cost one shilling and nine pence and the remaining threepence I would spend on bread. My mother would use half the rabbit with some pork trimmings and some of the potherbs to make a stew, and the next day she would make a rabbit and pork pie – the flavours of both dinners was just delicious.

My father's wages were roughly twenty one shillings a week. He gave my mother nineteen shillings, out of which she had to pay the weekly rent of eight shillings, so my mum had to work. When she was not well enough to work we were, as they say today 'on the breadline'.

★ ★ ★

One day my dad brought home a little buck rabbit and we called him Joey. Dad made him a hutch just outside the kitchen window so he could see us through the lace curtains. My brother Jack put a piece of blue ribbon with a bell round his neck and every time he ran it was funny to hear the little bell. One night my dad went to the 'Portland Arms' at the corner of our street to have a half pint, and he looked round to see Joey running along behind him. Whoever saw a buck rabbit waiting for his master outside a pub!

Some time after this my dad was out of work again as it had been snowing and there was no inside work for him. My mother had an attack of bronchitis so she was not able to go to the laundry to work either, and although my eldest brother and sisters sent home as much as they could afford, after paying the doctor's bill and the rent, there was little money left for food. On Sunday when we all sat down for dinner my mother put the large blue willow dish on the table, and on it was a lovely rabbit stew decorated all round with carrots, onions and false meat balls (which were made of flour and suet), and it looked splendid. But funny, both my mum and dad seemed very quiet and then we children looked at the dish then looked at each other and we all cried out "where's Joey?" One of my brothers ran out into the yard and lifted up the sack which covered the hutch and came back crying. "That's Joey" he said, pointing to the dish. We all looked over to where my dad was sitting shouting, "How could you be so cruel?" Without more ado my mum picked up the dish and carried it into the scullery. Poor Joey was wrapped up in the Sunday newspaper and put in the dustbin for deportation.

My dad said it was heartbreaking to have to do this and he vowed we would never keep pets again and my mother found an alternative for dinner. One of my sisters said "Is that all we have to eat?" I was very cross. "Why, would you have eaten poor Joey? Now he's to be eaten by the worms, how would you like to be eaten by worms?"

★ ★ ★

At one time our school gave out dinner tickets to the children whose fathers were out of work. The ticket consisted of a small piece of paper and our teacher put a rubber stamp on it with these remarks, 'LCC Dinner Ticket', name of the child and place to go and get your dinner. We then had to walk a quarter of a mile to St Peter's church, but before this we had to go home for a jug. When we got to the church we had to go down into the crypt where one clergyman dipped your jug into a big cauldron which usually contained lentil soup, and another clergyman gave you a slice of currant bread and a piece of brown, with no wrapping whatsoever. We then walked back home, scurrying along with our jug of soup and the bread and hoping that we would not be late back for school. The outcome was that half the soup was spilt and the other half was cold. I wonder what the present generation would think of that!

★ ★ ★

One day after school Keturah went back to the home of her friend Harriet, where her mother ran a shop and a coal business. Her mother suggested that Harriet might like some haddock for tea.

What about a nice 'addick over old 'Otts, all cooked with milk and butter?" (The thought of smoked haddock made my mouth water and I too was starving hungry). "Yes, I fancy a haddock; would you like one Ket?" and I said thank you and yes I would. Harriet's mother put her hand in her money bag that was tied round her waist and handed me three pennies. "Now go over to 'Otts and get a nice two penny one for Harriet and a penny one for yourself. Perhaps that gel of mine will eat it if you sit by."

But 'Otts didn't have any penny pieces, so I said "Just give me a two penny one please." "I got a three penny one here" said Mrs 'Ott. "No thank you" I said, and went back to tell Harriet's mother. "Oh never mind" she said "just give me back the penny." I was very disappointed as I was so looking forward to my piece of haddock. Harriet's mother then told me "You can stand and watch Harriet eating her 'addick, she might eat it if you stay beside her." I watched Harriet eat her haddock, my mouth watering, and I did hope that she would give me a piece of it, but Harriet ate it all and only left the head and tail. "There Ket, she only left the head and the tail. Would you Ket like to pick Harriet's ears and tails, they'll be nice and sweet? If you don't have them I'll only give them to the cat, but if you fancy Harriet's ears and tails you are very welcome." I stood for a moment and thought that perhaps the ears and tails did look tempting enough to pick over, but I said "No thank you, I'm not really hungry." Then I saw my mother come into the shop to get some coals and to look for me. "Mrs Fillimore, my Harriet has eaten all her 'addick, that's because your gel stood beside her. She only left the ears and tails. I told your girl she could pick over

Harriet's ears and tails anytime." My mother just smiled and said "Thank you."

On the way home I said that I really wanted Harriet's ears, but my mother's reply was "You don't want anyone's ears while you have two of your own."

There will be much more about spoilt Harriet and her indulgent mother further on in the book.

★ ★ ★

Most of the girls who came to our school often looked tired and sleepy, some were holding a piece of bread in their hands when they came into the classroom, that would have been their breakfast. I saw this many times and noticed that by ten o'clock in the morning half the girls were almost asleep. In those days there wasn't any free milk or anything to eat until we went home to dinner at twelve o'clock. I leave it to the reader's imagination as to what kind of meal that would have been, particularly for those whose fathers were out of work.[7]

Keturah, at this time a school monitor, recounts in some detail how she was asked to check up on possible pilfering in the girls' cloakrooms. She catches the petty thief red-handed and then has to decide how to deal with the situation.

---

7. It was estimated by a local headmaster of this time that forty per cent of the children attending his school were so poorly fed as to be unable to retain or profit by the instruction given them, while a further ten per cent were in an advanced state of malnutrition.

I went up to him not knowing what I was going to say or even how much bigger he was than me, and I thought momentarily that he could slip me one quite easily as we were all alone. "What are you doing here?" I said in a very dictatorial voice. "Come on, up on your feet". As I dragged him by his arms courage rallied around me which I thought I never possessed. The boy finally got to his feet and I was amazed to see when I looked down on him to see such a poor half-starved boy, and he seemed to have a very bad cough too. He told me that his sister was in Miss Jones' class and that she had told him where to find her coat hanging in the cloakroom, he was to come in here and would find two slices of bread and margarine tucked in her pocket. "I've done it before" he said. I held him by the arm and asked him why his sister had told him to do this, and he explained " My dad said I was to go without food until he came home from work tonight". "But why?" I asked, "come on, own up". "Because I took a penny out of mum's purse". "Why did you do that?" I asked again; by this time I felt like I had never been so important in all my life before. The boy coughed many times again and after that I saw how thin he was. "Come on, why did you steal a penny from your mother's purse?" "To have a ride on a horse at the fair" he said. "What's your name?" "Billy Watts." "Do you go to our school?" He nodded. "What's your teacher's name? And Mr Pond is your headmaster isn't he"? "Oh him, he's a rotten B... He gives you all the caning for nothing." "Never mind that Billy Watson, I must report what you have done to the headmaster, but I will do all I can for you. You can go now." As he ran down the stairs he shouted "I'll tell my dad and he'll come and bash you black and blue, and my mum too and all my mates, you'll have the biggest bashing of your life you rotten cow". My prestige fell quicker than it had been a few minutes ago, and I was afraid too. I didn't want to be bashed up. I had seen what boys did to other boys – they beat them until they were chased off by someone. I told our Governess what had happened and also Mr Pond the Headmaster. At a big meeting in the school I spoke up again for Billy, saying he was very hungry and that his father had forbidden him food, but the bread in his sister's pocket really belonged to his parents, so it did not seem he had stolen anything. He might have been sent to a reform school, but in the end he got let off with a caution. Mr Pond said he might not be so lucky next time.

I saw Billy Watts a few days later waiting outside school with a gang of boys. I thought what do I do now, and stood very still. They walked up to me slowly and the leader said "We ain't goin' to bash you up because you saved Billy from being put away." It was sure my lucky day.

* * *

Many of the men in our streets worked on the buildings as labourers when their was work to do, but in the hard winters I well remember the men walking up and down our street with nothing better to do. Without money or food there was nothing left but to go to the workhouse and a fat lot they gave them. By this time we were a family of eleven, so if it had not been for my mother working for countless hours every day we too would have fared very badly indeed. Fortunately we never had to resort to the workhouse for food, but some of my friends' mothers and fathers had to seek assistance in this way and my friends told me that this is what they received – a large loaf that tasted like chaff, one pound of brown sugar and one pound of rice. If you weren't at the workhouse by a certain time of the day you got the door shut in your face and someone would say "That will teach you not to be late".

★ ★ ★

Another important event was the joining of the Robert Browning Christmas Pudding and Turkey Club, which began in September. The night for joining was a special event for mothers and children as we lined up to join; (this mustn't be missed for anything). After waiting for what seemed an eternity my mother and I finally got inside the Robert Browning Hall where we were escorted to a long dark table where about six ladies and gentlemen were sitting. These people were volunteers whose primary duty was to take our particulars, like our names, addresses and requirements. The average people paid from three to six pence a week but most people paid threepence.

Two weeks before Christmas they gave out the pudding fruit to enable the mothers to make the puddings, then three days before Christmas they gave out the turkeys – the whole lot would have cost about seven shillings and six pence. How well I remember carrying home the turkey. There were long lines of children carrying them; the turkey was tied up with string around its legs then slung round our necks, feathers still on them were flying about our faces. I used to collect our neighbour's turkey too so I had two turkeys slung round my neck and I had some way to

carry them. I was exhausted when I got home but it was
worth the hard work to earn the four pennies.

The poet Robert Browning was born in Camberwell in
1812. In the same year he was baptised in the York
Street Congregational Chapel, later to become the
Robert Browning Hall. The hall became the
headquarters of the Robert Browning Settlement in the
mid 1890s, a centre for adult education, youth activities
and other works supporting the poor of Walworth. The
Robert Browning Hall is probably best known for being
at the heart of the drive to obtain parliamentary
legislation for Old Age pensions.

In 1895 there had been a government commission
to investigate the needs of the Aged Poor, and the final
report indicated the size of the problem, in that it was
estimated that nationally there were well over a million
old people in serious need. In 1898 an initial meeting,
attended by over 400 people, was held at the Robert
Browning Hall, to inform local residents about a
successful government pension scheme which was
operating in New Zealand. Subsequent meetings
continued to be held here for the next ten years, until
the Old Age Pensions Act received Royal Assent in 1908
and everyone over seventy was granted a weekly pension
of five shillings.

The Hall, built as a non-conformist chapel in the late
eighteenth century, was burned to the ground in 1978.

CHAPTER FOUR

Life in Walworth

Friends and neighbours; disease and public health; living and dying; Jimmy; funerals; the workhouse

Next door to our house was a forge and wheelwrights. Mr Benbow, the blacksmith, used to make iron rims for carts' wheels. I will always remember him for his kindness to me. He would often give me a drink of his tea which he had made in a beer can, and seeing as I had to pass the forge as I came home from school, he always looked out for me and nearly always gave me a biscuit with my tea. Sometimes I would blow up the furnace with the huge bellows, and when the fire was burning brightly he would put the iron into it, holding it with powerful callipers. When the iron was red hot he put it on the anvil to shape it into a round rim, banging away until he thought he had the right size. He used to say, "It must be right, it's no good having it too big or too small". One day he caught a chill and died of pneumonia. I missed him very much and remember how sad I felt when I walked past the forge doors which were closed for ever.

Keturah's best friend was a girl called Minnie, and she became very fond not only of Minnie but of her family.

Two houses away from our house I made a friend and her name was Minnie. Now Minnie knew everybody around the neighbourhood, and seeing that she sat next to me in school it's no wonder that I made friends through her, but she was my favourite. She was a small child with dark curly hair which hung about her shoulders. She looked so delicate, but her pale face and dark curls made her look so pretty. Minnie's mother had three younger children, her father worked as a labourer on the buildings, and like many other labourers, was often out of work during the winter months, so Minnie's mother and father were very poor.

Minnie's mother let the upstairs front room to a man and his wife, and Minnie's Granny occupied the front room downstairs, so Minnie's family had the use of the other two rooms. Minnie told me that her mother could not afford to keep the whole house which was rented at eight shillings a week, which was a lot of money in my days.

Minnie also told me that her Granny took in mangling at a penny-halfpenny a dozen; she told me that if my mother wanted any mangling done she could tap on Granny's window during the day and she would take it through, but not after dark, because Granny never had a light on because she was poor. Minnie also told me that her Granny had a "Box Mangle", which was like a big box-like thing with a flat top, and when she lifted the top cover there were two large wooden rollers which Granny would wrap round the clothes before she turned the big handle. The actual mangle had a ton of stones inside, I fancy I can see it now. Minnie told me that seeing the mangle took up half of Granny's room there wasn't any space for Granny to have a table, and no room for Granny to have a bed, so she slept on the mangle. "My mum" Minnie said, "put a small ladder to climb up with". I asked Minnie "Can't your Granny have a bed"? "There's no room, can't you see, anyway Granny's got an old armchair and there's plenty of room on top of the mangle". Sometimes Minnie slept with Granny, especially on Saturday nights, as her mother said she could not have her sleeping at the foot of the bed then because her dad got drunk on a Saturday night, "but only on a Saturday though", said Minnie.

Although Minnie was always Keturah's favourite friend, when Minnie left the neighbourhood, she made another friend, Harriet. However this was not such a close friendship. Harriet was a selfish child, while Keturah, the sixth of ten children, had a much more generous spirit. The two girls fell out more than once.

Harriet was an only child and I soon found out that she was very spoilt and could be mean. Sometimes she ate a whole bag of sweets and would then blow up the bag and pop it in my ears, laughing all the time. I really don't know why I did anything at all for Harriet. Now I wish more than ever that Minnie would come back.

One day in the playground at school Harriet came over to me. "Where do you live? I hardly remember you. Are you the girl that weighs up my mum's coals?" Looking down on me scornfully she said "You ain't very big are you?" "No" I replied, "and seeing that I can't see myself I don't even think about it." "Ain't your mum got a wardrobe with a looking glass in it so you can see yourself?" "No, we haven't got a wardrobe, but we have got a piano though and I would sooner have a piano than a wardrobe," "Well we've got both" said Harriet with a toss of her head. "Is your mum one of my mum's borrowers?" "What does your mum lend then?" I asked. "Money". "Money? Why does she lend money?" "Well if your mum wanted a loan at any time she could come and see my mum and if she thought your mum was a good principle she would lend your mother some money. So tell your mother that."

Harriet could have everything she asked. She had five big dolls dressed in lovely silk clothes, three dolls' prams, a skipping rope and three needlework boxes, one that played tunes. She was much taller than me and with her mass of fair hair and lovely blue eyes, she looked really pretty. Harriet's dresses were all made of silk or velvet in all colours of the rainbow; her mother made her a beautiful 'plum velvet' dress for Christmas and she also had new button-up boots with white stitching on. One Christmas morning Harriet knocked on our street door, and there she stood, just like a princess, and me with only a new pinafore over an old dress. For the first time in my life I felt envious. She said "Coming out Ket?" "Where?" I answered. "Round the houses". "I cannot, I have to help my mother cook the Christmas dinner". "Oh", she answered in such a disdainful voice, and with her head held high walked back towards her mother's shop. I shut the door quickly and did not give Harriet a look after, I couldn't bear to see her looking so beautiful and I vowed I would not be her friend any more. I passed her and passed her by many times; if only I had Minnie, dear Minnie, my true friend.

Harriet's mother, in addition to loaning money, owned a greengrocer's shop and sold coals round the neighbourhood; she was indeed a colourful character. One day Keturah had to bring Harriet home from school as she was unwell. They found Harriet's mother sitting on a chair outside her shop.

As she tried to get up off her chair she fell to the ground. " Here" she shouted, "Pull me up, come on Harriet, and you too 'gel". As I leaned down to pull her up I knew her breath smelt strongly of drink and I got a jolly good whiff of it, so much that I thought I had been drinking myself. Seeing that I had signed the "Pledge", I thought that God would think me a sinner. Harriet and I got her mum into the shop parlour and she fell down into a plush armchair. I made to go, but before I get the parlour door open Harriet's mum spluttered out, "Where do you live; ain't you Mrs Fillimore's kid? Yes, you have worked for me sometimes, haven't you? Come here, I can't see you over there. Of course I know you, your mother's got all those kids". Harriet said "She don't call her mother "Mother", she says "Mum", and I don't, don't I"? After a lot of struggling and staggering we closed the shop and then there was a shout from Harriet's mother; "Harriet, tell that girl I want her. Come here, what do they call you"? "Keturah" I answered. "That's a funny name" she said. After I had made her a cup of tea she dozed off, and what with the heat of the fire and the double gins she had over the 'Portland Arms', she began to snore. I saw Harriet had fallen asleep too so I tiptoed out in to the cold October air.

When Harriet was ill her mother asked me to give Harriet a wash. "I'm so fat I can't bend over her, you being so good, your mother has brought you up to nurse people. When you go home I'll give you some potherbs and a head of celery for your mother, and I'll give you a nice lamb bone, that'll make a good stew for you all. Gaud' knows, she can do with it with all her kids"

Harriet's mother (we never do get to know her name, as throughout her book Keturah describes her just as 'Harriet's mother') makes her next appearance at the Portland Arms when Keturah goes out one evening looking for her dad.

One night my dad went to have half a pint at the Portland Arms, this only happened perhaps two nights a week, (half a pint of ale cost a penny), and he was only ever a half hour gone, but on this particular night he had been gone nearly two hours. My mother looked at the clock, "Dad's a long time, I wonder what's keeping him". I offered to go see if he was alright, but my mother said "no, perhaps he has met up with some of his work mates and is having an extra drink, he doesn't often stay out". My mother was such a gentle person, she never made a fuss. We waited until eleven o'clock and in the meantime my mother had nodded off, she wasn't very strong now. I began to feel uneasy so quietly I put on my coat and as I walked up to the Portland Arms I could hear singing coming from inside the pub. When I looked inside, there was my dad and Harriet's mother dancing the hornpipe to a tune being played on the mouth organ by Mr Robinson. There was Harriet's mother holding up her skirts, up to her knees with her spring side boots in full sight of everyone, with her black shawl hung about her shoulders. And there was my dad, with Harriet's mother's hat on his head. They danced up and down the bar, and if it hadn't been for those circumstances, it would have been very entertaining. When they saw me standing at the door they stopped immediately and Harriet's mum went and sat down on the seat, very much out of breath, and I could see that she had had too many. "Hello Ket, your dad's a lovely dancer, him and me bin doin' the 'orn pipe. He knows 'ow to do it, don't you Jack?" (Jack? How dare she call him Jack.) I went over to where my father was sitting and grabbed Harriet's mum's hat off his head. "Now don't be rude", my dad said to me, "we were only having a dance, you know how I love dancing". "Whatever can you say to Mum?" I asked him quietly. Then Harriet's mother said "Nice girl you Ket, I could do with her, she'd be handy in my shop, what about letting me have her for good? Her and Harriet are real pals; I tell you what, Fillimore, I'll give you fifty gold sovereigns in your hand this minute". I stood dumfounded, but I had the good sense to know that she was a little tiddly, so I took my dad by the arm and led him home safely to bed. My father was very quiet for a few days after this affair, but as I knew it had only been in fun, I called in on Harriet's mum on my way back from school to tell her my mother knew nothing of the "Portland Arms affair", and would she be good enough to keep it that way; so all was back to normal.

★ ★ ★

Staying fit and healthy would have been extremely difficult in the Walworth area. Apart from most people being poor, houses were badly built, basic sanitary arrangements inadequate and many people were malnourished.

One of the dreaded diseases was consumption, because there wasn't any cure, and small pox too. But consumption was the worst I think. As soon as we heard anyone cough it filled us with horror and fear. One could see fine, strapping men reduced to skeletons, mothers and children too. When one heard that someone had been taken to the Brompton Chest Hospital people used to say that few people came out again, or they would be turned out, incurable.

One day my friend Minnie came to me crying "I've come to tell you that my dad is gravely ill and will never be able to work again, he's been turned out of the Brompton Hospital as incurable as there is nothing they can do for him". As time went by Minnie's dad sat outside his house wrapped in a blanket. Minnie used to cry when she saw her father drawing near to his end, "My mother won't be able to buy us food or pay the rent"; she knew where they would have to go after he died.

Looking back, it's no wonder that so many people had consumption, take for example the 'sinks'in the roads, the grids were so wide apart that you could see the stagnant masses of muck, which in the summer smelt dreadful. How well I remember when the council men came to clean the drains in our street. They used a ladle on a long handle, and after they had dug out the dirty muck it was put in a closed wooden van. The smell was awful, but it is true to say that the water cart man came along soon after and washed out the drains. There must have been all sorts of germs lurking there, no wonder scarlet fever and diphtheria were so prevalent, but they didn't have the 'know-how, like they do now in 1977.

We used to have real 'pea-souper' fogs in November, they sometimes lasted for days and you were nearly choked. You could smell it as soon as you stepped outside into the street, talk about pollution, with the soot, smoke and sulphur from the chimneys. There was a time when one of those 'pea-soupers' was at its worst when a man lay dying of consumption in our street, somebody else caught small pox and my best friend Minnie had pneumonia. It was said that if you could live for nine days with pneumonia, a change would take place, either for the better or the worse, many times it was for the worst.

I remember Joe who lived in our street; I watched him growing thinner and thinner until he looked like a skeleton sitting on a chair. I used to cry and say to my mother "Can't you do something for poor Joe?" "No my dear," my mother would answer "when he's an angel he'll be better." "Well why can't God do something?" I asked. "It will be many a year before a cure is found for that disease, if ever" she said.

When Joe died there wasn't a penny of insurance for his wife as he had been ill for such a long time. I was in Joe's house when a man from the Parish called and this is what I heard him say "Do you want your husband to be buried by the Parish? It will only be a rough wooden coffin, no varnish, no handles, just plain wood. And your children can't come and here's a ticket for the workhouse food." But in our street we could not see Joe buried in such a fashion, so my mother and I went round the houses for a collection and we collected enough money for Joe to have a proper funeral. How eager I was to see Joe's varnished coffin which had four lovely brass handles, but it wasn't long after this that Joe's wife and family all had to go to the workhouse. That was a sad day for me especially as I felt so powerless to do anything.

★ ★ ★

From an early age Keturah was made aware not only of the process of childbirth but the subsequent plight of many mothers. It was common for families to have ten or more children. Keturah herself supported her own mother through several pregnancies.

"It seemed that there were always babies being born in our neighbourhood, and it seemed that my mum was always being called to help. Her services were free of charge and she always took her own toilet requisites, including her own towels. The doctor used to come to our house and ask her if she could lend a hand. "There's a confinement on the way" he would say, and she never refused. After the baby was born she used to wash mother and baby before she went to the laundry, and I would clean up the house and give the other children their breakfast before taking them to school. I used to be in my school desk by nine o'clock so there was no time for self pity, you just got on with the job.

One night in the depths of winter, I remember it was raining in torrents, there was a knock on our door and when I opened it a man said "Is your mother there? Mrs Filmer? My mother came to the door and he said "Could you come along and help me? It's the first house past the forge you know" he said, pointing to the house. "It's one of those two what's going up steps. I'm a doctor from the Parish, you know, the workhouse, only there is a young woman in labour, could you help?" My mother asked "Is she the young woman who sells watercress in the market; she's a hunch back isn't she?" The doctor hesitated before replying that this was so. My mother told me to bring the jug and basin, soap and towels and Jean's clean nightdress, and the baby powder box with the powder puff.

The house we went to had three floors. We had to go to the top flat which was just two small rooms, the middle floor consisted of another two rooms and a lavatory on the landing, downstairs there were two more rooms. The people who lived in the top and bottom flats all had to share the one lavatory. When I arrived with all the articles my mother needed I saw this poor, hunch back, slip of a girl lying on a straw mattress, heavily in labour, with no fire or heat of any kind. The room was dark and damp and lit only by a candle and a lantern. I went home to make a jug of tea and collect some little cakes my mother had made, but when I arrived back at the flat the baby had been born. The doctor and mother enjoyed the hot tea and cakes, and then the mother and baby were taken to the workhouse to continue her confinement. I still find it difficult to believe that this really happened.

The poor got poorer and the mortality in childbirth was

appalling. I can recall seeing sickly babies in the doctor's surgery, their mothers pale and worn through lack of good food and having too many children. It was a familiar sight to see a little white coffin under the undertaker's seat awaiting burial. What a state of affairs, there seemed to be no change in life, no way out. Mothers having babies, fathers out of work, no out-of-work pay, no nothing.

Keturah, still herself a child, was well aware of the dreadful conditions in which families were living in her locality; her own mother had lost three children as infants and a fourth would die before he was two years old. She would not have known however that slowly, very slowly, the high infant mortality rate, in particular in big cities, was falling. From 1870, when infant mortality was 15%, to the 1930s, when it had dropped to 7%, conditions were beginning to improve. Change would happen through many strands of educational and social development; women would become more literate and aware of family planning options, they would learn how to provide a healthier diet for their families, and the local councils would start to pull down the badly-ventilated small houses and ensure that the water was cleaner. They would also improve sanitation.

Charlotte and John Filmer had their own painful experiences of losing children. Before Keturah's was born three unnamed babies died at birth or soon after, and baby Jimmy failed to thrive, dying on his second birthday. Keturah wrote a poignant account of the life, death and funeral of this little boy.

When I was eleven my mother had another baby and she named him Jimmy, I really don't know why Jimmy, I imagine that she had run out of names. By the time he was four months old my mother and I agreed that he was not making progress like our other babies, somehow he didn't look right, he never cooed or smiled, he didn't start to look round and take notice, so we took him to the Children's Hospital. The doctors said that they would not be able to tell us anything until he was between six and nine months old, but they did think that there might be something wrong with his brain, and this made us all very sad at home. At a further visit to the hospital there was a baby specialist in attendance and he reaffirmed that the problem was with Jimmy's brain, but went on to say "Mother, if the baby's brain develops he will be a genius, but only time will tell". So all we could do was wait.

As time went by Jimmy was always in his cot in our kitchen and we children used to play with him, but all Jimmy could do was look up now and again, he never took notice of anything. I liked to take him out of his cot and nurse him and sing to him, and somehow I felt he knew me, somehow we seemed able to build our own friendship and communication. This went on until he was nearly two years old; when I called his name he would open his lovely blue eyes and move his little mouth, but no word ever came out. Then one day a diarrhoea epidemic broke out in our area and one of my brothers got it, then Jimmy. After he had been ill for a week the doctors said there was no hope for him, but Mum and I took turns sitting up at night with him, attending to changing his nappies. Then there came the Saturday morning when there was suddenly a shout from Jim, "Mumma, Mumma"; the shock of this caused me to knock over a pail of water which went running all down the passage. I rushed over to Jimmy's cot and my mum rushed in from the scullery. "He's spoken mum, he's spoken, he called "Mumma" twice. When we looked down on him his beautiful eyes were wide open, he gave us a wonderful smile and then he passed away, just like that. When the doctor came and my mum told what had happened he looked puzzled; "Perhaps if he hadn't caught the epidemic his brain would have developed and he could have possibly been a genius". To this day we will never know.

The neighbours came in, together with my school friends, sympathising and wanting to know if they could do anything. Mrs Muffery said she would wash him. "I like to make them nice and clean before they go to the angels" she said, making the sign of the cross. I thanked Mrs Muffery for her offer, but said that my mum would like me to wash Jimmy. My mum nodded sadly saying that I could do this for her. I could not bear anyone else to touch him. Jimmy and I had been such good friends in his tiny world, I could not desert him now.

My mum got the water and towels ready and I washed him and put on a clean nightgown and then carried him gently to our small parlour on a crisp, white pillow. I did this so carefully, he looked so peaceful and I did not want to disturb him. I laid him on our small black mahogany table and covered him with his lovely white shawl which my dear mum had crotcheted for him a few weeks previously, and then I burst in to tears. I quickly dried my eyes as I did not want the younger children to see me cry

41

and then made the neighbours a cup of tea. Before they went home I took my friends in to the parlour to have a last look at Jimmy.

During the weekend everyone seemed very quiet and sad. My dad cried, the first time I had ever seen him cry, for he was a tough man, but always a pillar of strength.

On the day before Jimmy's funeral I had an accident at the swimming pool, slipping on the wet tiles and banging my head on the marble floor. I just about managed to get home, but I knew nobody was in the house as Mum and Dad and the children had gone to buy Dad a new bowler hat to go with a dark suit a neighbour had lent him for the funeral. I must have then collapsed into unconsciousness as the next thing I knew was I was in Guy's Hospital with my mum and dad, tears running down their faces, and three doctors, all standing round my bed. My dad said "Thank God" when the doctors said I could go home. We travelled home in a 'box wheeler'[8] and my mum put me in to her bed. When we were ill we always were put in my mum and dad's bed.

Jimmy's funeral was on Friday, but I was still in bed and not well enough to go. My mum made some lemonade and cakes and my friend Elisa came round with her violin. Then the vicar arrived and we sang 'There is a Green Hill' and he spoke of little children who had gone to God and suffer the little children to come unto me, so really the day passed happily.

---

8. Box wheeler – Despite internet searches and contacting both the London Transport Museum and the Tyrwhitt-Drake Museum of Carriages in Maidstone, I have been unable to find a precise definition of this vehicle. Commonly known as a 'growler', it is most likely to have been a four-wheeled version of a hansom cab, more suitable for older people and families. The hansom was a two-wheeler, a superior vehicle, faster and lighter and of great appeal to the young and fashionable. Taximetre cars (petrol-driven cabs) began to appear on the streets in 1908. The 'wheeler' was also the name for the lead horse when two were driven in tandem

★ ★ ★

When Minnie's Granny became ill and died suddenly, her uncles came round at once and asked Minnie's mother if Granny had left any money. Although her mother thought there was no money, the uncles thought there was, and wondered if it was in the mangle. Granny had not yet been buried and was lying on the mangle, so the uncles lifted her off and laid her on the floor and broke up the box mangle, but they didn't find anything. Minnie told me that Granny wasn't insured so a friend went round the houses asking neighbours to subscribe towards Granny's funeral. I asked her how much money was collected and she told me five pounds. "Will you have a new dress?" I enquired, but Minnie said "No, my mother is going to put a black armband on our arms and she has to buy a black cap for my dad and my uncles. By the time the funeral tea is paid for the money will be all gone".

My parents allowed me to go to Granny's funeral and I must say I enjoyed Granny's last day on earth. I looked out of the carriage window and waved to my school friends, then there was the lovely tea and winkles and bread and jam. I went to bed that night in high glee and hoped the next event would be just as enjoyable – but I did miss Granny very much and when I passed her window I always took my hat off in respect.

A few days after the funeral I was sitting with Minnie in Granny's room when her uncles came in, saying they were sure she had some money. Quite by accident one of the uncles knocked over Granny's armchair and then they saw that there was a small black velvet bag tied to one of the chair legs; the uncles made a dash to get to the bag first and when they opened it they found a few golden sovereigns. They all shouted "Now we are rich" and made step to the "Portland Arms" at the corner of our street to celebrate. Later they came back with bottles of beer and cider under their arms singing "Rule Britannia", and they sang until it was all gone. Granny's savings soon went that way.

From an early age Keturah had come to understand the importance of an appropriate funeral for the departed. For the very poor, like Joe, the funeral would have had a very simple occasion, but for the better off, like the street-traders, there were all sorts of opportunities to exhibit your wealth to the neighbours, even when you were dead! What follows Keturah wrote as if for a script for a play – it is a poignant example of high-pressure salesmanship and also perhaps of keeping up with the Joneses.

Another time I was in a school friend's house when the undertaker called to make arrangements for her father's funeral. Now my friend's father had been a prosperous street trader so there was plenty of money about. I will now relate the conversation I heard between the undertaker and Mrs Reed, the widow,

Undertaker – "Sorry to hear of your great loss Mrs Reed, so sudden too". Mrs Reed – *(nods her head)* Undertaker – *(solemnly)*"I don't like talking about these things, but it's the arrangements for your dear husband's funeral. *(he hesitates)* Yes, it's about the arrangements, how many carriages will you require? You see Mrs Reed, you have a lot of relatives. Right, I'll put down four carriages. *(writing in his notebook)* And it's lucky Mrs Reed, we've just had some new ones in – they'll be nice. Now, *(leaning over towards where Mrs Reed was sitting)*, now how about the plumes? You know, plumes for the 'orses 'eads, would you care for them?" Mrs Reed had, it seemed, no option but to agree. Undertaker – "I'll tell you, we've just 'ad some lovely mauve 'orse draperies that hang on either side of our specially trained, docile black 'orses. What with the plumes and the velvets, it will make a lovely show, seeing as 'ow your husband was so well known - *(he went on slyly)* he would have agreed I'm sure." Mrs Reed – *(whispering)* "Yes, yes." Undertaker – "Yes, Fred was a good man, wasn't he Mrs Reed?" Mrs Reed – *(bursts in to tears)* Undertaker – "Now, how about mutes? Wold you like the mutes to stand outside your door before your dear husband is carried out? Right, I'll put you down for two mutes. They stand on your top step opposite each other. Alright Mrs Reed? Funny, I've just engaged two mutes, the best in the business. Do you know what Mrs Reed?" Mrs Reed *(looking over to where the undertaker is standing)* "No." Undertaker – I 'ad to sack the other two because they was always late and when they did turn up they couldn't stand still, which is the most important thing they 'av to do. Been at the bottle I shouldn't wonder. Alright, I'll put you down for two mutes, for I know before your dear husband is carried out he would have been pleased with them I'm sure. We never know what is before us do we?" Mrs Reed by this time seemed quite uninterested as the undertaker makes his way to the door. Undertaker –

"As I was saying, the other two mutes I 'ad, you know the ones I was telling you about, well I had just bought them two lovely second-hand bowler hats, only a bit bashed in. Well you know the band of crepe we put round the hats, well they both 'ad a lark and turned their flat bowlers back to front so the crepe bands hung down over their faces. "To make the kids laugh" they said. Laugh? I don't pay them to laugh. Well, I'll say good day and I'll put you down for the two mutes. I'll be here two thirty sharp on Thursday, trust me to be on time."

The day of the funeral arrived and I took up my position at the bottom of the slip so I was certain of getting a good view of the two mutes and to see the horses with all their ornaments. I remember saying to my school friends "Are the mutes alive?" They had white powder all over their faces and looked as if they had all the worries of the world on them. I was more interested in the mutes than anything else. I liked their flat bowlers with the band of crepe, and what with their long faces (their bowlers had fallen down over their ears) and their long coats buttoned up from top to bottom, and their black gloves, I had never seen anyone looking so gloomy in all my life.

I was so engrossed in the mutes that I nearly missed the coffin coming out. The floral tributes were amazing. There was a huge cross on the coffin with these words written on a card, 'Gone and not forgotten. Your loving wife Mable', and then there was a vacant chair from the children to 'Dear dad'. The funeral procession began to move away at a very slow pace with the undertaker walking in front, and we watched until it was out of sight.

As I was walking home I began thinking about the lovely tea the mourners would be having when they returned from the cemetery and I began to conjure up in my mind what excuse I could make to knock on the door of my friend's house, hoping I would get invited to tea. I found that excuse and enjoyed that excuse and when I got home I told my mum and dad how lovely the tea was. "Trust you to be there" my dad remarked, but he made me put in the dustbin the funeral lily which had fallen from one of the wreaths, he said it was unlucky to bring it into the house.

* * *

On the night of Minnie's father's funeral I cried myself to sleep. It was some time afterwards that Minnie's mother had the 'Broker' in, because she couldn't pay the rent, and then she was turned out of her house and they all had to go to the workhouse. It was about twenty minutes away from our house and when we got to the workhouse Minnie clung to my arm, "I will die there, I know I will". My mother had offered to take Minnie to live with us, but the authorities said that the children must not be parted. At the workhouse gate I could only console Minnie by saying that I would be waiting outside the next day for us to go to school together. This was heartbreaking and to this day still lingers in my mind. I saw Minnie back to the workhouse for a short time and then one morning she didn't come out. I heard that she had been taken to an orphanage. I missed her very much.

An outstanding period in my childhood was when I

was old enough to realise the plight of the poor men and women, so many really were destitute. The aged people, unless their children could support them, had a very bad time. The parish gave very little indeed, there were one or two other charitable institutions, but they fell short from anything worth mentioning so it was no wonder that a lot of the poor souls had to go to the workhouse.

I used to go, together with my school friends, and stand outside the workhouse on Sunday mornings and wait for the old folk to appear, Sunday being the only day they were allowed out. Our purpose was to give them little wraps of sweets and biscuits, it wasn't much we had to give as we had so little ourselves, but my word, weren't those old men and women grateful, real thankful.

The old folk used to come out in single file and then branch off, men on one side and women on the other side of the road. Why they did this I never knew. The women were dressed in a plain blue serge dress with a linen apron, and I recall a black oval stamp on the front of the apron, which I imagine showed the name of the workhouse, and they had spring side boots and a black bonnet and shawl. The men wore dark blue serge suits and dark caps. The old folk would return later in the day and I could see tears running down their poor old wrinkled faces. Another Sunday would seem a long way off for them.

I always came away from seeing them back to the workhouse with tears running down my face, and I vowed that my mum and dad would never go into a workhouse. I also vowed that when I was old enough I would try to alter this distressing state of affairs, but what could a small girl do in this great big world? I think that it was about now when I started to wonder about my own chances when I left school. I was just eleven at the time, only three years before I too would have to go out into the great unknown.

From information given to me by the Southwark Local History Library it would appear that the local workhouse to which Keturah refers would have been Newington St Mary, in Westmoreland Road. The neighbouring hamlet of Walworth had been constituted a Poor Law Parish in 1836 and was overseen by an elected Board of eighteen Guardians whose role was to ensure that there was sufficient accommodation and work for the poor of the parish. The workhouse was built in 1850 and housed male inmates in the east side of the building and females in the west; in the centre there was a dining area, laundry and kitchens. In separate buildings were sick wards, lock (venereal) wards, a mortuary and casual wards for overnight vagrants.

As with all admissions of children the boys were separated from their mother and had to have their hair cut short and to wear workhouse uniform.

After 1930 the laws governing workhouses changed and St Mary's became known as Newington Lodge Public Assistance Institution under the control of London County Council.

It is of interest to note that in 1896 Charlie Chaplin, later to become a star of the silent screen, along with his half-brother Sydney and his mother Hannah, was admitted to this workhouse for a few weeks.

Happier times

Hop picking; May Day celebrations; Empire Day; Easter Day; The Band of Hope; Sir Ernest Shackleton visits

The highlight of my young days was in September when most of us in our street went hop picking in Kent, for apart from a day now and then at the sea-side in the summer, there was nothing else to do. But going hop picking was something to be reckoned with, all my friends and myself could talk of just nothing else but going to the lovely fields in Kent and we looked forward to the farmer's letter to say he could accommodate us. We went by train at midnight; it was called the 'Hoppers' Train' and left from London Bridge. We were all packed in so tightly in the carriages that the air soon became hot and foul mostly from the smoke of the engine, but also because some children were sick or couldn't get to the toilet in time, so there were streams of water everywhere.

In spite of this cheap service we all arrived safely at our destination, so it was well worth the discomfort of the journey to smell the freshness of Kent's beautiful air and see the harvest moon shining on the green fields. That was just wonderful, but sleeping in barns on straw palliasses certainly did not appeal to me very much! We cooked our food in hopping pots outside our barns on the green and by six thirty in the morning we were off to the hop fields where we all helped to pick hops into our mother's hop bin. During the day the farmer's boy came round with warm fresh milk and how we gulped it down, for London children this was a real treat.

We did not go to the hop fields on Saturday and Sunday afternoons, instead we sat on the green and sang songs to our heart's content until bedtime. Then it was time to go back to our barns where we children slept like tops on the clean straw till the morning.

The hop picking season lasted for four weeks and by then the children's faces had been transformed from a pale white to a beautiful bronze. At the end of the picking time we had to pack up all our things ready to return to those not-looked-for grimy streets where we continued to recall the lovely fresh air and mountains of sunshine.

★ ★ ★

I now come to another highlight of my young days and that was the first day of May. I was not alone in my excitement as most of the girls in my school looked forward to that day and the sunshine. Curiosity mounted as to who was going to be chosen to be "May Queen" and her twelve "Maids of Honour". After several weeks of waiting finally a girl was chosen, not by our teachers, but by the Borough Councillors and the trustees of the Robert Browning Hall. My teacher put my name forward many times, but somehow I never got on the list and I was always disappointed when my name was not called, but I did have a lot to do with the preparations. One of the things I did was help make the white dresses for the chosen girls; I would sew to my heart's content, still hoping that one day I might be the May Queen, but for now resigned to my fate.

At six o'clock sharp on May morning the Council's horse and cart would come and pick up the May Queen together with her Maids of Honour from their houses. I sat with the driver after helping the May Queen on to the high chair in the cart which was surrounded by small chairs for the Maids of Honour. The carts were bedecked with lots and lots of spring flowers and bunting and the horses were draped with lovely coloured ribbons and had rosettes on their harnesses.

Then it was time to move off – what delight! By now the crowds were beginning to gather and they all joined in behind the cart as it drove through the streets of Walworth and the main roads in the Borough. What a wonderful sight to see the crowds of children and grown ups lining the streets at this time in the morning. Finally the procession arrived sharp at eight o'clock at the Browning Hall and the Queen dismounted from her chair and was the first to enter the hall.

What a lovely girl she looked. She wore a wreath of spring flowers on her head and had a white dress, white shoes and white stockings. She held a beautiful bouquet of flowers and looked so radiant in the early morning sun. Behind her followed the twelve Maids of Honour who then lined the entrance for their Queen, before they all made their way slowly forward to the stage which was decked with more spring flowers and a big Union Jack. My duty was to see that all the girls were seated on the stage ready for the press photographers. After the initial ceremony there was hymn singing and prayers and then it was time for tea and buns – you bet I dived in there, I was always looking for food! Then it was time for the Queen and her attendants to be escorted back to their homes in order to get changed and be at school by nine o'clock.

Looking back I remember the delight of this day, what a pleasure to look forward to after the long, cold winter. I attended this occasion every year until I left school, and eventually, when they were old enough I used to take my own children to see Robert Browning's "May Queen". (Thank you Robert Browning).

★ ★ ★

Just three weeks after the crowning of the May Queen, Keturah was celebrating again, this time May 24th, Empire Day, a very important day in the British calendar at that time.

A week before May 24th we were all busy at school making red, white and blue rosettes, and rehearsing hymns and patriotic songs. We held the celebrations in the Boys' School playground and Mr Pond the headmaster used to open the school gates so that passers by could stand and watch us. One year I was delighted to be chosen as Britannia. I sat on a blue chair in the middle of the playground surrounded by all the flags of our Empire. My teacher played the piano for me whilst I sang 'Land of Hope and Glory', and if I am not blowing my trumpet too much, I had a powerful voice and could sing and recite very well.

After this was all over we went into the Boys' School to have currant buns and hot tea, which was provided by the teachers. Then we children played games like 'Postman's Knock' and 'Kiss in the Ring', but always under the watchful eye of the teachers of course. This was a special treat for the girls to have the boys with us, because we were usually kept well apart! I think I liked boys' company better than girls. I thought girls were such weak things. I loved playing boys' games like football, swimming and yes, believe it or not, I liked boxing. My dad used to say boxing wasn't for girls, they are only there to produce sons!

Empire Day was established in 1902, one year after the death of Queen Victoria in honour of her memory. One of its aims was "To remind children that they were part of a British Empire and that they may think with others in lands across the seas, what it meant to be sons and daughters of such a glorious Empire." At school the children would hear stories about the heroes of the Empire, like Robert Clive and Cecil Rhodes, and learn patriotic songs and salute the flag.

Empire Day was an essential part of the British calendar for over fifty years, particularly for children when they had time off school for marching, maypole dancing, concerts and parties. With the decline of the Empire after the Second World War, when new political alliances were developed and independent countries wished to celebrate their own identity, Empire Day began to smack of Imperialism. Political correctness won the day when in 1958 the name was changed to British Commonwealth Day and by 1962 the date had been changed to November 2nd and the name to Commonwealth Day.

The time of year I much looked forward to was Easter time, and Good Friday was simply wonderful. Firstly the hot cross buns. On the Thursday evening my mother put threepence on the table for me and at seven o'clock on Good Friday morning I was off to the baker's shop where I bought twelve spicy hot cross buns, all for threepence. I was very tempted to eat one on the way home as the smell of buns was right under my nose, but that would not have been fair so I resisted the temptation.

On Easter Sunday morning my mum put a lovely Easter egg on the table that she had made for us all and on Easter Monday my friends came knocking at the door to show off their new Easter dresses. The material was called 'crushed strawberry', a shiny red material just the colour of a strawberry. Their mothers had struggled all year to be able to afford to buy the material and they had made them themselves, every stitch. My mother used to make the boys shirts and knit their pullovers, and me, one year I had a navy blue skirt. We children were pleased with our new clothes and Easter passed happily.

★ ★ ★

Another highlight of my school days was belonging to the

Band of Hope which was held in the 'Little Mission Hall', known locally as Dunns Mission, near the market. I went to meetings on Fridays after school where we had hymn singing and prayers and the minister showed us lantern slides, mostly about poor children in far-off countries. I did sometimes wonder if he thought us poor children were better off. Once a month the minister gave us buns, and we always ended the meeting with 'Twinkle, Twinkle Little Star'; when all was over the minister would stand at the door and shake hands with us all saying 'God be with you my little ones'.

In the early part of the year Dunns Mission gave a 'Robin's Dinner' for the children who were members. One year my school friends got to hear about this and asked if I could get them a ticket, but I told them that unless they were members they could not go. One of the boys then said "We'll join the Band of Hope if you can get us a ticket". "If I can get you a membership there are certain rules that you have to swear to keep" "What rules?" they all wanted to know. "Well, first you must say your prayers every morning and help others that you see in trouble. Then you must sign the pledge stating that no strong drink will ever pass your lips."

They all looked at each other and agreed between them that they would keep the rules, saying "Across my heart" in one voice.

As they were leaving I stopped them saying "Just a minute, you haven't heard all yet, it's a penny to join, because the mission requires the pennies to go towards the tea and buns and also the Robin's Dinner." Lenny asked "Can't we pretend that we have paid our penny?" Harry just said "I'm going to walk in, I don't care about your minister, he's for God ain't he?" They began to walk away so I called them back "Let's talk it over, I think I know a way. On Saturday morning I work for Harriet's mother, the greengrocer who sells coals; if you want a job you could take the coals on a trolley to the customer's house, and you will get a penny each time, and sometimes Harriet's mother might give you a carrot, that would be nice wouldn't it?" After hearing this they all agreed, except Harry who said "My mum won't let me do this, I bet she'll say I'll wear my shoes off my feet." After some hesitation we all agreed to pay his penny out of our coal money. I might add that I didn't need a ticket as I was classed as an 'entertainer', so I gave my ticket to my brother who was not a member. I used to sing 'Annie Laurie' and 'Onward Christian Soldiers' and recite 'Jack and the Giant Killer' and the lovely poem by Robert Browning 'An Incident of the French Camp'. After the "Robins' Dinner" I seem to remember that the attendance at the Band of Hope meetings dropped off.

The Band of Hope was founded in 1885, one of many temperance groups set up at that time to counteract the influence of pubs and breweries, and also to provide activities for young children to encourage them to avoid the influence of alcoholism. Today the movement has been transformed into Hope UK and is mainly concerned with children's welfare.

Now a Mr Shackleton was due to make an appearance at

the Browning Hall after one of his Antarctic expeditions. I asked as many school friends as I could muster to come after school and line up outside the Browning Hall to give him a welcome. As I was the leader I lined the girls up on either side of the doors where he would make his entry and there we waited for what seemed to be an eternity. By this time the grown-ups had started to arrive to see the explorer and started pushing us out of our places, but I called out "Stay where you are girls, we were here first, don't move." By now the queue was a quarter of a mile long, but we girls held our forward positions. Finally we heard the rumble of a box wheeler so we started to clap our hands and wave our hats, and those who did not have hats waved handkerchiefs.

The box wheeler stopped and out came the explorer. He wore a black overcoat with a beaver collar all round it and a black bowler hat. Just at that moment the big doors were swung open which I wasn't prepared for, and I fell into the hall. I soon picked myself up and the man who opened the door let me and my friends stand just inside the entrance to the hall, so we had a grandstand view of the explorer. When he entered the hall I held out my hand for him to shake, but he looked down at me and touched my head saying "If this doesn't deserve a bun I can't think of anything else." Then he told us we could sit in the two front rows for his lecture. I must admit we girls didn't understand much of his lecture about his expedition, but when we caught sight of the hot tea and buns we were the first to get to the table. We went home munching buns all the way.

Ernest Shackleton, the polar explorer, was the third officer on Captain Scott's Discovery Expedition (1901-4). He returned to the Antarctic in 1907 as leader of the Nimrod Expedition and in 1908, on his Great Southern Journey, reached the furthest south latitude yet, only 112 miles from the South Pole.

On his return to England Shackleton was feted as a public hero and knighted by King Edward the Seventh. In order to help pay for future expeditions, he undertook a strenuous series of public appearances and lectures, such as this talk at the Robert Browning Hall.

CHAPTER SIX

Keturah's schooldays

King and Queen Street School; Miss Biddy - teacher training; recruitment for swimming lessons

Although Keturah makes no reference to her early days at school it is clear that all children of school age used the same building. This was King and Queen Street Elementary School[9], an eight- storey building on the edge of the market; the youngest children used the ground floor, the senior boys the second floor, the senior girls the third floor and the playground was on the roof. The head of the Girls' School was Miss Drew, but Keturah usually refers to her as just 'Governess'; Mr Pond was the boys' headmaster, and she describes him as a diminutive man of just four feet eleven inches.

I fancy I can see him at the school gates. He always wore a tall 'Hard Bowler' hat, I never saw him without it. But could this man control the boys? I never saw better. If the boys deserved the cane, he gave it, with no regard for what the mother or father did. This was brave of him as ours was a very tough neighbourhood.

9. King and Queen Street School was renamed Robert Browning School in the nineteen thirties. The school still operates from the same buildings. Keturah had passed by her old school a few years before and she commented that it had been built to last and looked none the worse for wear.

Minnie and I went up to the Big Girls' school together. How well I remember that morning. When we sat down in our new classroom I got Minnie a seat next to me and we waited for the teacher to come in. It wasn't long before she made her entrance. Minnie whispered to me "I don't like her much, she looks a misery." "Well try to like her" I whispered back. "Well I shan't" was her reply.

Our teacher's name was Miss Biddy. She wore her hair, which was turning grey, with a big bun which was twisted round at the top of her head. She had little squinty brown eyes and when she looked at you through her glasses it seemed she had no eyes at all. She was very strict and was soon slapping the girls on their hands. I remember thinking I hope she doesn't slap me as I would not have known whether to laugh or cry. However she made us work hard at our lessons and to spell too. On Monday morning she would fill the blackboard with all kinds of words and there on the blackboard they stopped until Friday afternoon when she would rub them off with her blue duster.

One by one the girls would have to call out the words that had been on the board and we would have to spell them and it was woe betide anyone who spelt the words wrongly. She would say "You haven't been singing the words as I told you to. You will never learn to spell if you do not sing them." And the same went for arithmetic, history and geography. For all her hard work, by the time many of the girls left school at fourteen years, they still could not read or spell very well.

Keturah was probably fairly accurate in her observations of Miss Biddy's inability to help children to learn. In the lady's defence, she undoubtedly cared for her charges, even if her methods of discipline were somewhat heavy handed, but she probably would not have had the necessary skills to teach effectively and would have been satisfied if she could just keep her large and unruly class under control.

Some teacher training colleges had been set up in the early part of the nineteenth century, most associated with the Church of England, but it was not until 1846 that a pupil-teaching scheme was launched for selected elementary schools, such as Keturah's.[10] This scheme allowed thirteen-year-old children to be apprenticed to a school for five years, with the head teacher giving an hour and a half's instruction every day. Students would then have the opportunity to take the Queen's Scholarship examination. Those who passed could move on to a recognised teacher training college and become a 'certificated teacher'. Many young people chose not to take this option and carried on teaching, maybe like Miss Biddy, as 'uncertified teachers' or 'pupil-teachers'.

Many middle and upper-class children of this period would have been taught by university graduates in small private schools, endowed grammar schools or public schools, but the majority of these teachers would not have received any specific training.

10. Keturah herself may have been heading down the pupil-teacher route when she was thirteen. She refers to a time when she had been teaching the girls in the lower class for several months during a teacher's prolonged absence.

The first university-sponsored teacher training course was set up in 1890 when 'day training colleges' began to be established, and by 1902, with the passing of the Balfour Education Act and the setting up of County Council Education Committees, the training of teachers became integrated into the adult education system. The pupil-teacher training system was phased out by 1907 and replaced by a scheme whereby young people could stay on at school until they were eighteen and then proceed to a teacher training college once they passed the entrance exam. Today all teachers are required either to complete a three-year degree course in education or a one-year post-graduate course.

Swimming was a great love of mine when I was at school. The London County Council engaged instructors to work in the schools around south London and one day Miss Biddy got our class together to talk about us girls having swimming lessons. "Now hands up those who would like to learn to swim." Out of about forty girls only about six put their hands up. "Why girls, don't you, and you and you" she said, pointing at various girls, "don't you want to learn to swim? What about you Hestor, surely a big girl like you would like to go swimming?" "Well, the water will be too cold" replied Hestor. Another girl said that she worked at a wet fish shop, and besides "swimming might catch me a cold and cause my death, and I earn a shilling a week out of which I give nine pence to my mum, and that helps her buy the potatoes." Miss Biddy shook her head in dismay "Now Eliza, what about you?" "I have to do mum's housework and look after the babies." "Babies?" Miss Biddy asked, "how many babies?" Eliza counted on her fingers "One, two and twins six months old." "Is your mother ill then?" Miss Biddy asked. "Oh no, she works at cleaning the classrooms after we go home." "Can't you find anyone to mind the babies, or perhaps we could make the time earlier and that wouldn't upset the baby minding." After some hesitation Eliza said "Even if my mum said yes, my dad wouldn't let me go, he would say I'd catch me death on me lungs." Miss Biddy was getting frustrated and looking over to Violet said "Wouldn't you like to learn to swim?" "Yes, Miss Biddy, but seeing as how I wouldn't get home until a quarter to five, it would be too late." " Too late for what?" asked poor Miss Biddy. "Well my dad's blind and I have to take him to where he stands on the main road. I have to see that his card is on straight and is the right way up; it says 'Remember the Blind'. I also have to see his mug is secure round his neck, so I couldn't come, I really couldn't, for he earns a few pennies this way."

Life was hard in those far off times, but Miss Biddy did eventually manage to find some girls who wanted to learn to swim and we enjoyed our swimming lessons and I became a very good swimmer and won a good few prizes and certificates. (I might add that some of my certificates ended up patching the ceiling!)

CHAPTER SEVEN

Family connections

*Pride in a family name; Keturah's plan to save her family;
the Filmers of East Sutton Park*

Although John's line of the Filmer family (from
Otterden) branched off from the main Bearstead line at
the beginning of the seventeenth century, becoming
yeoman farmers some eight generations before he was
born, John passed on to his children a sense of pride in
his family name and in the fact that at one time his
forebears had been gentlemen. Keturah knew this, as
did all the children in the family, and she also knew that
nearby to their father's Bearstead birthplace, the
original Elizabethan mansion at East Sutton Park was
still standing and was still inhabited by the titled line of
Filmers. Keturah illustrates her own understanding of
her relationship to this family in a conversation at school
with Miss Biddy.

I was always a bit of a favourite with my teacher and one
day she called me out of class. "Keturah, seeing as how
you are so reliable I shall want you to mind the class for
half an hour this afternoon. I know that I can trust you to

Townley Street, Walworth, where the Filmer family moved to in 1900
(The Book of Walworth 1925)
Photograph kindly supplied by Southwark Local History Library

The Filmer Family at Harry's wedding – June 1912
Back row – Jack, Harry, Noel
Middle row – Keturah, Clara, John, Charlotte, Annie, Margaret
Front row – Walter, Jean, Thompson (Tom)

Harry, John and Jack, who all served in France in the 1914-18 war (family archive photograph)

The May Queen and her attendants ("Eighteen Years in the Central City Swarm", Herbert Stead) Hammond - 1913
Photograph kindly supplied by Southwark Local History Library

A COSTER'S FUNERAL
'(WALWORTH).

PART OF THE PROCESSION.

A Coster's Funeral, Walworth ("Living London" 1903)
Photographs kindly supplied by Southwark Local History Library

Newington Workhouse
(photograph kindly supplied by Southwark Local History Library)

Scouts of the 2nd Walworth Troop with Scoutmaster Marsh on the Thames above Blackfriars Bridge – 1912

Thompson (Tom) Filmer, aged 12, at the helm
(Photographs from the Betty Lashmar collection)

Funeral of the Boy Scouts who were drowned off Leysdown

"The Mourning Scout" – Memorial to the lost Scouts at Nunhead Cemetery
Photograph kindly supplied by the Scout Association

Walter Filmer aged 17
(family archive photograph)

Keturah Filmer and
Will Daveney, c 1916
(Family archive photograph)

keep the girls quiet. By the way, why did your mother give you such a lovely name, it's so unusual?" "Well Miss Biddy, it's a family name, my dad's family came from a very important family and some of them live in a mansion at East Sutton Park in Kent. They even built their own church in the grounds, and back in time some of them were great scholars and writers." Miss Biddy then asked me "Why on earth do they not help your father, it's their duty". Without hesitating I said "One day Miss Biddy, they will send us a letter for us all to go and live with them." "I hope they will not be too long in sending for you. What name did you say?" "Filmer" I replied." "The same as yours?" "Yes, my dad said that he was a third cousin."[11]

It was not long after Keturah had helped her mother at the confinement of the young hunchback girl that she began to appreciate even more keenly the plight of the very poor and homeless. She also started to consider the reality of her own family, locked in to their life of poverty, and wondered what, if anything, she, a twelve-year-old girl, could do to facilitate change.

I never forgot that young mother and her newborn baby being taken to the workhouse, that scene made a great impression on me, and it was this that helped me to make up my mind. Somehow I was going to go to the Filmer mansion at East Sutton to ask for help to get us all out of our surroundings. Enough is enough.

11. After three hundred years and some eight or nine generations, the relationship was actually not quite as close as John described!

I worked in Harriet's mother's shop for a whole week during one of the school holidays and for this she gave me half a crown [12p]. It was a new half crown. I had never had a half crown to myself in all my life, so I hid it under the lino in my bedroom. This was to be the most important item in my plan. I went to London Bridge station to ask the times of the workman train. "Where are you going?" the ticket collector asked. "To Maidstone." "All by yourself?" "Oh no, I'm being met off the train when I get off the train at Maidstone." "That's alright then. Be here at twenty minutes to seven any morning."

On this Friday afternoon I walked down the stairs from my school and I stood looking at my school thinking that this could be the last afternoon I would ever see my school again, for on the morrow I had made my plan to catch the workman's train to Maidstone. I found out that there was a bus from the station to East Sutton and I began to imagine my arrival at the mansion. I would knock on the mahogany doors and inform whoever opened the door that my dad was a third cousin to them and that we lived in a back street in south-east London. I would tell them that we are now only a family of five children as my older brothers and sisters are away working. I could not think of anything else to say at this time, but I would think of the rest to say on my way down there.

On Friday night I gave myself a good wash, dressed myself and put my nightdress on over my clothes, for I must be up at half past five the next morning to walk to London Bridge station to catch the workman's train. I told my plan to one of my brothers, who was two years older than me, and he said "You'd better not, you will be missed before you have been gone five minutes."

I rehearsed my plan, like not forgetting to take my half crown from it's hiding place, and creeping downstairs and shutting the front door very quietly, for one false move would ruin everything, I could not afford for a thing to go wrong. Before I got into bed I said my prayers and asked God not to fail me and to wake me at half past five, for this would mean the world to me and to my family. We could move from this house to where there are trees and green fields, I could have a bedroom with a dressing table in it, as could my brothers and sisters, my brother Tom could have a pony and a stable and then he could give his old wooden horse to some poor little boy… and I fell asleep.

Suddenly I heard my dad calling me, "Come on. Get up quickly." "What for, what's the time?" "Never you mind, get up," he went on as he went downstairs. "Get dressed right away" he shouted. Little did he know that I was already dressed. I sat down on a chair and wondered whatever it was he wanted me to do. "Go put two kettles of water on the gas." I thought whatever does he want with two kettles of water? My dad still had his back to the fire which I could see had been newly lighted. "What's the matter Dad, is anything wrong?" "You'll see", was all he said. Then everything began to dawn on me. "My plans" I almost said aloud. "This is my day for the great secret, oh God, what has happened?"

I heard the clock strike six o'clock and I am still sitting in bewilderment when there was a knock on the street door, then another, and when I opened it I saw Mrs Lambing, the woman who attended confinements. "Hello" she said. "Why have you come?" I asked as she began to walk upstairs. "Don't you know?" "No, I don't." "Well your mum will have a baby very soon." "A baby?" I cried out, "My mother is going to have another baby?" "Don't say you didn't know, you go around enough with your mother in confinements." "Yes" I answered back, "but my mother do not charge." "Don't be saucy" she said, and upstairs she went to where my dad was with my mother. I sat down and cried, all my plans had gone to the wind, never could I hope to have any plan again. I looked at the daylight coming through the window and I fancied I heard the workman's train coming in to London Bridge station, and in my girlish way I thought my happiness had gone for ever.

Another knock at our street door. "Good morning lassie." It was Doctor Sanderson, now I knew that all this was true. Whatever did my mum want another baby for? Why didn't she tell me? Soon the doctor came downstairs; I knew him well, he always came to our house for my mother's births. "He's a lovely little fellow" he said, touching my head. "You'd better go up and see what you can do for your mother." And he shut the door behind him.

After a while Mrs Lambing made her departure and my dad got himself off to work. I could not believe that we had another baby that I would have to mind. This was her fourteenth, now we are ten in the family and my mother is forty six years old. Sadly I went upstairs. I knew now that we would always have to live here in this house, I could see no hope of improvement, same winter or summer, and when I left school what would I do? I didn't know and I didn't care.

Slowly I went into my mother's bedroom and saw that they were both fast asleep, so I tiptoed downstairs to prepare my mother some breakfast. When I went into her bedroom with the breakfast, which consisted of a cup of tea and a lovely soup plate of Quaker Oats with lashings of milk, she awoke and smiled at me. "Sorry I didn't tell you." I looked over to our new baby,[12] he yawned and opened his eyes, then off to slumberland as he began to get used to his new surroundings. "What shall I get for dinner mum?" this being Saturday morning. "If I go along to the market I'll get an oxtail and make a stew." She raised herself up with some difficulty and I shook her pillows and made her comfortable. "Did Dad leave some money?" I asked. "No, he had to walk to work today because he will not have any money until he comes home at twelve o'clock, so we must wait till then."

She dozed off again and I saw that this last baby had taken a lot of her strength. I tiptoed across to my bedroom and saw that my youngest sister Jean was still asleep. I quietly got my new half crown from its hiding place and stood by my dearest mother. "Close your eyes" I said. We used to play these games if anyone had a surprise. "Now what have you been up to?" I took her hand and put my half crown into it. "Open your eyes." "Wherever did you get this from, it's a lot of money, now you must tell me."

I told her the whole story and she said "We'll keep it a secret and who knows, one day it may come true."

★ ★ ★

12. This baby was named Walter Eric and was the author's father.

If Keturah's plan had succeeded, maybe she would have knocked on the great door of East Sutton Manor and been welcomed into the house by a butler or housekeeper and then shown into the library or drawing room to meet the tenth baronet, Sir Robert Marcus Filmer. Keturah may have known a little about the house and some of its past residents, but would no doubt have been very excited if Sir Robert Marcus had offered to show her round his grand home and tell her more of its story and his family. It is an interesting story and just a part of it is worth retelling here.

The senior branch of Keturah's family were landowners, living at Otterden, a few miles east of Maidstone. In 1610 Sir Edward Filmer and his wife Lady Elizabeth moved into the recently-built Manor House at East Sutton. They produced eighteen children, ten surviving into adulthood. After their deaths, their son Robert commissioned a commemorative brass which can still be seen today in the little church alongside the Manor House. The brass depicts Sir Edward and Lady Elizabeth with their eighteen children, nine girls and nine boys, and is said to be one of the finest brasses in the country. In the previous century an heraldic crest had been approved, this depicting a golden falcon rising from a broken golden castle. The associated motto was from Virgil, '*Nescia fallere vita*', which can be loosely translated as 'A life ignorant of deceit'.

Sir Robert inherited the estate in 1629. An ardent royalist, he was also a local magistrate and officer of the county defence force. During the time leading up to the start of the Civil War in 1642, he wrote a book, *Patriarcha – a Defence of the Natural Power of Kings against the Unnatural Liberty of the People*, which justifies the King's absolute authority and his divine right to rule. Although this book was not published until 1680, Sir Robert became a marked man and Cromwell's soldiers would have kept a close eye on his movements. The Manor House was under fire several times and the house ransacked and Sir Robert was finally arrested in 1643 and imprisoned in nearby Leeds Castle until 1647.

Sir Robert's health deteriorated during the time he was in prison, but on his release he continued to support the royalist cause by helping royalists with their plans to escape to France and America, until his death in 1653. It was during this period that the Filmer family fortunes began to take a downward turn, lesser members fell by the wayside and the social gap between the East Sutton Filmers and the rest began to widen.

Keturah's own ancestors were descended from a family of comfortably-off farmers. In 1757 one Edward Filmer married a farmer's daughter, Keturah Apps, from whom her father was directly descended, but by his death, records indicate that Edward ended his life as a farm labourer. So the downward trend continued.

Fast forward two hundred years and we meet up again with Sir Robert Marcus Filmer, who in 1884 became the tenth and last baronet at the age of eight. Robert Marcus was a soldier, serving in the Grenadier Guards in the Sudan and South Africa. At the outbreak of the First World War his regiment was one of the first to go to France, where Sir Robert was awarded the Military Cross for Gallantry for bravery whilst fighting near Neuve Chapelle. Sadly Sir Robert died of wounds in 1916. Leaving the front line trenches he discovered that he had left behind his pince-nez glasses in his dug-out. Returning to retrieve them, he was fatally wounded, and with his death the baronetcy became extinct.

After the death of Sir Robert Marcus much of the East Sutton estate was sold to cover death duties. From then on the Manor House was only used at weekends and for shooting parties until 1939 when the house, now no longer a permanent residence, was requisitioned by the army and the Royal Artillery moved in for the duration of the Second World War. In 1945, after the war ended, East Sutton Park was bought by the Home Office and became the first open Borstal in the world. The house is now a women's prison.

A few years ago I was given a guided tour of East Sutton Park and discovered that despite the necessary adaptations to the building, it is still possible to have some sense of the original Elizabethan manor. When you walk into the wood-panelled entrance hall, you see a beautifully-proportioned stone fireplace, stone floor and wooden carved ceiling, all unchanged since Tudor times. There are many rooms with superb carvings and sculptured ceilings and the initials E and E can still be clearly seen carved in stone on either side of the dining room fireplace and also in oak in the main hall. If Sir

Edward in his doublet and hose, and Lady Elizabeth in her embroidered gown and beaded head-dress, were to have walked down the main staircase, somehow I would not have been surprised!

CHAPTER EIGHT

Looking towards
the great unknown

*Careers advice; East meets West; Keturah's last day at school;
learning to make buttonholes*

I was now thirteen and starting my last year at school and
still had no firm ideas about what I might do when I left
school. However one day Miss Biddy called the older girls
together saying "I want all the girls who will be leaving
school to stay behind after school today so that we can
have a discussion about what sort of job you have in
mind." We all sat round her table and Miss Biddy began
to address each girl. "Hester, what sort of work might you
do when you leave school?" Hester hesitated "Haven't
thought about it," was her reply. "Now Lizzie, what about
you?" "Well I can clean doorsteps for threepence a step."
"Cleaning door steps, how do you mean, what do you
do?" Miss Biddy asked. "Well we scrub the door step first
and then we make a nice half-moon with the hearthstone[13]
and it dries lovely and white, that is unless the kids don't
tread on it before it dries," Lizzie explained. "What if it
rains for a week?" "'You will be out of work for a week and

13. A soft stone used for whitening hearths and doorsteps.

that means you won't have any threepences. "Now Keturah, you must have something you want to take up, surely." "Well Miss Biddy" I said, "we girls haven't really had a chance to think about this, for we have never been away from this part of London, except when we went 'hopping'. We have lived and played in the streets all our school life, we do not even know what the West End of London looks like." "Do you mean to say that not any of you girls have ever been to the West End of London?" When no hands went up she said "Unbelievable." Then she went on "Why didn't I think of this before, sheer neglect on the part of the school." "Oh we don't blame you or the school Miss Biddy" I said, "but it's not too late for us to go now, is it?" "Oh indeed it isn't" replied Miss Biddy "I will tell you what I will do, I will speak to the Governess about this, and girls, I will then tell you what we intend to do."

A few days later we had another such meeting round Miss Biddy's table. "Now girls, hands up who would like a situation in domestic service, we know of many families who would employ you. You would first be trained for housework by the housekeeper of the house, and then you could work your way up to become a housemaid." "Would that mean leaving home?" asked one of the girls. "Yes, but you would get one evening off a week and every other Sunday after you have washed up the luncheon dishes. Now hands up, who would like that?" Not a hand went up. Then Rosey said "I'm sorry Miss Biddy, but I wouldn't like to leave home." "Oh dear, then what about needlework, like working a sewing machine, but unfortunately most of those jobs are in the West End of London." Miss Biddy hesitated and then went on "I'll tell you what I will do, I will take you to the West End tomorrow and we will call into some shops and see if we can find you girls a good job. Yes Keturah, I see your hand is up, what did you want to say?" "Do you think it would be better if we girls went to the West End on our own, that would perhaps give us the confidence we need? If you tell us exactly the way to get there I feel sure that we could find our way, with your instructions of course – and there's always a policeman to ask." Miss Biddy was a little surprised at what I had proposed. "Well Keturah, yes I think it a good idea and you can write a composition on your first look at the West End of London. Well I think that's all, unless you have any last minute thing to say."

But there was one more thing to ask which Miss Biddy had not considered, and that was, who was going to pay for the day in London? "Miss Biddy" I said, "we can't go without money and I'm sure my mother could only give threepence to go." Turning to the others I said "What about your mothers, how much could they afford to give?" Most of the girls thought their mothers could only pay a penny. I turned to Miss Biddy, "Isn't there a fund you could call upon, some special fund I mean Miss Biddy?" Miss Biddy was beginning to say that she did not know of such a fund when the Governess came into our classroom. When she learned of our plight she called Miss Biddy aside and as she left the room she said "Good luck girls on your adventure tomorrow and take care of yourselves. If you get into any difficulty there are plenty of policemen to ask." Miss Biddy was smiling all over her face which made a change. "Good news girls, good news. Governess is giving each of you one shilling and sixpence out of her own pocket, this will enable you to have something to eat and pay for your fare to the West End. What wonderful news and how pleased I am that you are going. Now how many of you are there? One, two, three, four five, that will be five times one shilling and sixpence. I'll go and get the money now."

When she came back Miss Biddy said "Who is going to take care of the money?" and all the girls said "Keturah". So Miss Biddy put the three half crowns in an envelope and sealing it up said to me "Now Keturah, you are in sole charge of the girls and the money, a big responsibility, but you Keturah can take it." Thanking Miss Biddy for her kindness and the Governess for her money, we walked home talking excitedly about the morrow.

Next morning we five girls started off at nine o'clock. What an event this would be for us. We walked to the Elephant and Castle and took tickets on the Bakerloo Railway[14] to Piccadilly Circus, taking care to watch every station. In my handbag, which my mother had given me, I had a pencil and paper together with the money. "Be careful" my mother had said "and do not speak to anyone except a policemen."

At last we saw the sign on the station, 'Piccadilly'. We stood outside the tube station in amazement not knowing where to go. "Look" I said "there's a tea shop down that side street, let's go." Without further ado we went into the tea shop and when we saw the cakes filled with 'Real Cream' the card said, we just could not wait. "Five of those cakes please." I asked for, "and five cups of tea." The

14. The Bakerloo Railway was originally the Baker Street and Waterloo Railway. Opened in March 1906, it was officially renamed the Bakerloo Railway by that July, with popular support. The line was extended to the Elephant and Castle Station by August of the same year.

waitress looked at me very suspiciously, "Where's your money?" she said. "I have it in my handbag." "Show me. That's alright then. Go and sit at that table. That will be five pence for the tea and seven pence halfpenny for the cakes." The waitress asked us what we were doing in this part of London and when I told her that we were all looking for jobs for when we left school, she directed us across the road towards a big shop. "Tell them that Molly from the tea shop sent you."

My four friends and I crossed over the road carefully – so this really was Piccadilly. Bewildered, we looked through the big swing doors of the huge shop and tentatively walked inside. "Look" I said to Rosey, "look at those lovely dresses". Rosey went up and touched one, but Eliza stopped her. "Don't Rosey, you might get us in a row." We moved on to another counter. The notice read 'Lingerie'. I looked closer at the word and asked Liza if she knew what it meant. "Never seen that word before Keturah," she said. We moved along the counter looking through some glass cases where there were some beautiful underclothes. Rosey asked Eliza if people wore them. "Well if they don't wear them, what do they do with them?" she replied. Rosey said "I'd catch my death if I wore them."

We then walked on to another counter where there were women's blouses of many colours, some with frills all down the front and on the sleeves. How I wished that I could have bought one for my mother. I told Hester that she would look lovely in one, with her black raven hair, but the price ticket read four shillings and eleven pence [23p]. However could I afford that amount of money? "How many doorsteps would I have to clean to get enough money to buy one of those blouses for my mother?" I asked Hester. "A good many Keturah!" she replied.

We then came to a counter where the card read "Silk Scarves". They were hanging up in dozens all the colours of the rainbow. I imagined that I could feel that silky material round my neck. They were one shilling and eleven pence each. "So money buys all these lovely things" remarked Eliza. We began touching them, they were just irresistible. "Real silk" I said to Mary, who hadn't said a word since we entered the shop. I looked at her and saw that she was deathly white. "I feel sick" she said, and before I could do anything to help her, she was sick all over the counter. "Oh goodness" I cried, "whatever can I do?"

At that moment a gentleman came up to us. He was dressed in a black coat and striped trousers, and looked very important. "What in the world is this? How dare you come in the shop front? Sight-seeing I suppose". I was still propping up Mary with my hand over her mouth in case she was sick again. "Look here" the man said, looking down on me. "You had better go outside, and be quick about it." "How can I? You can see my friend is sick. Have you got anywhere where she can sit down?" "Kids" he said to an assistant at the scarf counter. "Didn't you see them when they came in? You should have turned them out. We can't have this sort of business. I bet you know where they come from. Sticks out a mile doesn't it? Get the boy to clean up this mess Miss Tremmer, and you, Miss Bailey, take these, (pointing to us) to the cloakroom and give her a glass of water, then send them about their business, and see this never happens again." He gave me a push saying "Off you go."

I stood there in defiance. "Excuse me sir, you are much mistaken about my school friends and me". "No time to listen to silly bits of girls" he said. I made him listen to me. "We are not silly girls, we are on a school mission. This is the first time that we have ever been to the West End of London, we live in the south-east." "You don't have to tell me that, I can see it" he said. "That's good sir" I answered. "It would take me some time to tell where you come from." "Good heavens, good heavens," he raved. At that moment a lady came out of her office.

"Anything the matter Mr Phillips?" "No, not really" he answered. "Kids from over the water." "Alright Mr Phillips, I'll attend to this child" and she drew me aside. "What's the trouble?" she asked. Then I told her that we were on a school mission and were wanting to find a job when we left school, and that we had to write an essay on this our first day in the West End. "I see, it's just a misunderstanding, you see this entrance is for customers only" she said, pointing to the doors we had come through. "Follow me to my office." "I understand, but where to we go to ask for a job?" With a smile she said "Come along, it's round the back where you will see a card in the window saying 'Employees Entrance', I'll show you. Do you know," the lady said as we were walking towards the 'Employees Entrance', "when I was your age I had to come in to this very entrance to obtain a situation. I was thirteen and a half years old then." "Did you live in the West End?" I asked her. "No dear, I lived in south-east London" she said smilingly. I felt that I could have been her friend for always.

When we got back to her office she said "When you and your friends leave school come straight to my office and I will take you to the employment office where I hope we will be able to find you work. And there's one other thing you should remember through life, and that's a proverb, do you know what a proverb is?" "Yes, like 'Look before you leap'," I answered. "Well, not quite like that, but always remember, 'It's not where you live, it's how you live'." "I understand" I said. She then took me took me to the staff cloakroom where to my amazement all the girls were having a wash and brush up, including Mary, who was by now fully recovered. We were then given some refreshments from a special table all laid out with sandwiches for us. What an enjoyable time we had and somehow we had a sense that our future was secured.

We spent the rest of the day window gazing and watching the fine ladies being helped out of their carriages by the uniformed doormen of the big and beautiful shops. I must say that my mind that day was filled with both curiosity and gloom. I knew we had to go back to Walworth and at the same time I realised that it was only money that could buy all those wonderful things. And why, with only a few miles between us, should there be such a great divide in the way of life? People in south-east London worked very hard, but received little reward for their effort. Both my mother and father worked tirelessly to bring up their large family, they never asked for support nor did they expect it. These days (1977) they would have been eligible for child benefit money, but not a penny piece did they receive, whether they were sick or well, they had to rely entirely on themselves.

★ ★ ★

I have now come to the last afternoon of my schooldays, and I can still remember this so well, it is as if it was yesterday. My teacher, Miss Biddy, gave a party for me in the main hall to which all the girls in the school were invited. When we were all assembled in the main hall, for me it was a tearful scene, a time of saying goodbye, because I was now fourteen years of age. My teacher had tears in her eyes, my special friends Hestor, Eliza, Mary and Harriet were also in tears although they too would soon be leaving school. My teacher played and sang 'Auld Lang Syne', then all the girls sang 'For she's a jolly good fellow', and Miss Biddy gave me a present, a little white Bible. Governess gave me a silk handkerchief with my initials on it, there were flowers from other teachers and each of my friends gave me remembrance cards which they had made themselves.

When the final departure came I asked my teacher if I could leave the hall alone. I could not bear to have anyone walking down those stairs with me. I wanted to walk down the stairs for the very last time all alone except for my thoughts, and this I did. So tearfully I walked from the hall with my arms full of presents and flowers, alone and slowly. Usually I would run down the stairs two at a time, but this afternoon was different. Slowly, down and into the street, without looking back at my old school, that would have been too painful. This was one of my saddest days, (except for Jimmy), for I was about to enter the great unknown.

I had to find a job, but what kind and where? Was I going to perhaps work in Piccadilly? I knew that my mother and father would always try to help me solve my problems, I could always put my faith in them, for both were a tower of strength. I had heard my mother say to my father on my fourteenth birthday "Our family is almost grown up and left us." "But" he answered, "we still have four more to bring up and we are both getting older." It seemed that they realised the big responsibility they beset themselves, so much uncertainty and so little money to feed us all. But they always struggled on, bless them.

After an exhaustive search of my memory I have now come to the end of my schooldays reminiscences. All I have written is authentic and I hope is interesting to read.

★ ★ ★

Keturah, with the help of Bessie, her sister-in-law to be, did find employment as soon as she left school. Bessie was a head machinist with H. M. Rayne, Theatrical Costumiers, and she was able to secure Keturah a job in the workroom in the Boots and Shoes Department.

H. M. Rayne's factory was in Waterloo Road, almost opposite the station. The front entrance was in Waterloo Road and the factory entrance was up a little side way. It was in this factory that beautiful suits and dresses, boots, shoes and hats were made for the theatre, music halls and pantomime. The window displays showed off dresses and suits made of satin or other stylish materials, like silks and georgette, or other shimmering materials. Top hats were often made of the same materials with boots or shoes to match. It was really delightful to see all these beautiful clothes adorned with pearls and diamontes, shining in the coloured lights when the windows were lit up at night.

I was very nervous on my first morning at H. M. Rayne. Bessie told me a few things as we walked along, but I still felt rather bewildered. "What kind of work will I have to do?" I wanted to know. "You will sit at a work table beside a girl named Molly, she will tell you everything you need to know" Bessie reassured me. The department I worked in was called 'The Boots and Shoes Department' and this was where the machinists machined the uppers of the footwear and the girls on the work table stitched the buttonholes by hand, all ready for the men to put on the soles and heels.

The first thing I had to learn was how to hand stitch a buttonhole and it was Molly who showed me how. First I was given a piece of linen with the buttonholes already cut out, then I had to hold a piece of fine cord (called 'gimp') round the edge of the hole and work the buttonhole stitch over the top. No 'gimp' must show when the stitching is finished. Molly then explained what I would have to learn next. "When you can sew perfect buttonholes you will work buttonholes for satin boots or shoes, and the piece of satin you work on is called a 'fly'. For High Boots you might have eight buttonholes to stitch. When you are done you hand over the 'fly' to Bessie and she will sew it on to the uppers which will be then stitched on to the boot. Do you understand?" I answered "Not yet, but I will eventually."

After three months of practising sewing buttonholes, Bessie came over to me and took my 'flies' for the Forelady, Lottie, to see. "Perfect. Now give these green satin 'flies' for Keturah to work the buttonholes; the order is wanted urgently for the start of the "Puss in Boots" pantomime, and mind you don't prick your finger, because if a spot of blood gets on the 'fly' it is spoilt." Thankfully all went well and I watched Bessie sew the 'flies' to the green satin boots' uppers. Now I was a professional buttonholer and I was very proud.

Lottie now wanted me to learn a new job, dying ribbons to match the boots or shoes, as she said I had a good eye for colour. So now I was also a professional dyer of ribbons for which I got a rise of one shilling, making my weekly wage four shillings and sixpence. Time went on happily and I had worked at Rayne's for over a year when one day, when I was working with Molly, laughing at one of her jokes, she gave me a sudden kick under the table. "Stop laughing" she whispered, "Mr Rayne has just come in." I got on with my work but could hear his footsteps coming nearer and nearer, and then he put his hand on my shoulder saying to his lady secretary "This is the girl." I thought I was going to faint, he must have seen me laughing and I would get the sack. "Stand up and take your overall off" he demanded. I stood up, my legs shaking. "Follow us" he ordered as the whole room went silent. I walked behind them through the room and down the stairs into the big office and then through to the front shop where the secretary said "Follow me into this office." It was Mr Rayne's private office. "Sit down girl and Miss Fisher will tell you what all this is about" and he went out of the office.

"My name is Miss Fisher" she smiled. I expect you are wondering why we have called you into the office. Just a minute" and she rang the bell for tea, "with an extra cup as well." Then in came the tea and Mr Rayne came back, drank his tea and told me that Miss Fisher would explain everything, and he left the office again. Miss Fisher sat down behind the polished oak desk, "Mr Rayne has brought you down here for me to tell you that he thinks you are just the girl who later on, when I retire in a few year's time, has all the potential to take my place, you'll be old enough by then. You have a fine personality, you speak beautifully in a businesslike way and your appearance is just what is needed. I will train you myself, but first you will work in the big office under Mr Binny to learn office routine, then you will work in this office. At times you will go with 'Master Willie' to the warehouses to learn how to buy materials and to learn how many shades there are to say pinks, greens, yellows, mauves. You'll be surprised how many shades there are to one colour. Now, have you anything to say?"

I was naturally surprised and was unsure how to reply. "I thank you for everything you have said, but I do not think that I have the intelligence for this 'Place' you have given me in your office, and besides, I am very happy upstairs in the Boot and Shoe Department with the girls on the table." "Oh my dear, your confidence will come as time goes on. Now, how long have you been with the company?" "Just a year Miss Fisher," I replied. "Mr Rayne says that you will make a fine business woman, he has great hopes for you. Now you can go home for the rest of the day, we have had your hat and coat brought down, so you can go out this way. Please tell your parents all, and you are to have a half crown a week rise." I thanked Miss Fisher for giving me such a wonderful offer and said "I will work hard to live up to the heights you have bestowed on me."

As time went on I grew in confidence and learnt quickly and within a year was able to do all that was asked of me. Miss Fisher said that Mr Rayne was very pleased with my progress. Then one night when I came home from work my mother was in bed. She had had a heart attack. The doctor was with her and wanted her to go to hospital as she was going to need long nursing, but my mother said she would fret in there. I knew at once what I must do. "Doctor Smith, I will look after her." "But you have an important situation, you cannot sacrifice your job, it's yours for your working life." "My mother is my life" I said, "it's just like going from one situation to another, besides there are my brothers and sister to look after, so I have made up my mind right away." "You're a good young woman" the doctor commented.

I wrote to Miss Fisher telling her the sad news and thanked her for her kindness to me, but I knew that my mother and family needed me. Bessie took the letter for me and told me how sorry both Mr Rayne and Miss Fisher had been. It was such a pity. Miss Fisher said to Bessie "Such a promising career has been sadly ended, on the other hand, Keturah was such a person and we would have expected her to do this. Her mother and family must come first."

My mother did slowly get better, but never fully regained her strength. She remained a semi-invalid for the rest of her life.

CHAPTER NINE

Improvement and progress

Family developments and thoughts about the future; Noel the fire-fighter and the Romans; Westminster Abbey and a long walk home; the family photograph

By the time Keturah was coming towards the end of her schooldays the five oldest children had moved away from the family home. Harry was working his way through a seven-year printing apprenticeship, Annie was in private service, Clara learnt court dressmaking for a while and then moved away to be a forelady in the north of England, Margaret, a very go-ahead person, became a housekeeper in London hotels, but was also an expert needlewoman, a wonderful cook and also a professional hairdresser.

All my older sisters were now engaged to be married and my brother Harry also announced his engagement to a young lady named Bessie and they planned to marry in 1912. We were now all growing up. I was considering becoming a nurse, Jack loved dress making. He used to make doll's dresses and sell them for threepence each and was determined to be a dress designer when he left school. Noel however was very different to any of us, he was always imagining rescues at sea. "First overboard I'll be and bring the drowning man aboard". He read a lot of books about sailing ships and my dad used to say "Noel will make a fine man when he grows up, a man of the sea". Mother just commented "We never know what is front of us, we'd better wait and see". Tom was interested in following the family tradition of printing and Jean said she was going to be a ballet dancer. Noel laughed at that idea, "She's skinny enough" he said.

Writing about the younger group of children still at home, Keturah gives a sense that at last life was getting easier, perhaps the hard times really were over and the younger members of the family could enjoy their life together. The never-ending worry about money also lessened when John at last found regular employment – what a huge relief that must have been.

One day my dad came home and said that he had found a permanent job so my mother need not go out to work anymore. Good news indeed. Then we were able to move to a new double-fronted house, still in the Walworth area, but opposite a swing park. It had three nice bedrooms, a sitting room, a dining room, so that the Chippendale furniture and the piano looked lovely. My dad built a kitchen out in the garden and also a bathroom from a big shed. He bought a dining room suite too, so our wooden

chairs were put away under the stairs for us to take when
we married.

Keturah now reflects on the ever-changing relationships
within her growing family and remembers with pleasure
the enjoyable times they had together. She recalls some
family activities and notes in particular how Noel, now
fourteen, and Tom, twelve, were growing up.

We were a very happy family. Clara and Margaret were
married, Harry and Annie engaged, there were no money
worries and everyone was doing well, what happiness,
what more could we want? We sometimes got together as
a family and enjoyed musical evenings together, my dad
had a fine baritone voice and we could all sing. At this time
rag-time was coming in so I also enjoyed going dancing
with my girl friends and some of the "Browning Boys". I
particularly liked one of the young men, he had lovely
auburn hair, but all the girls were looking in his direction
so I knew I stood no chance.

Noel had been working in a solicitors' office for some
months now. On his fourteenth birthday my dad bought
Noel a silver watch and chain, Harry gave him a brief case,
my mother gave him a smart worsted suit and his boss
bought him a bowler hat. It was a delight to see him going
off to the office in the mornings and his boss said he was
progressing very well indeed. Noel was Tom's great friend
and Noel was so good to him. Tom thought that Noel was
the only one in the family and he never did anything
without asking Noel's advice. "Noel" he said, "will be my

great friend for life", and this was true. Whatever Noel did, Tom did. If Noel did not like rice pudding, Tom did not either!" Tom, was doing very well at school, coming top in many subjects and was still hoping to follow his grandfather into the printing trade.

One day I asked Noel if he had found a young lady since he'd been out at work. "Plenty" he answered, "that is, going to and coming home from work." "With your good looks I expect you'll be bringing one home soon" I observed. "Maybe" he answered. "You're pretty quiet Noel. They'll have to be pretty good for Noel Faulkner Filmer" I went on. "Well yes, I do have a girl" Noel said "and if you do really want to know" he went on, with his usual air of confidence "her name is Charlotte Ellen Filmer." "Don't be daft Noel" I remarked, "you can't marry your mother." "Who spoke of marriage Kit, I didn't. I tell you here and now, I'll never marry while mother is alive. When I have saved up enough money I will buy her a cottage in the country." "Where?" I asked. "Mother once told me that she was happy when she lived in Bearstead, that's where. She deserves everything I can give her." Tears ran down my face, why hadn't I thought of this as well? "Mother has had a hard life" he went on, "and I will do everything possible for her." Tom was following Noel's footsteps, I did not think he would ever be a leader, but with his placid nature, he would be a good second. Walter, now four, said that he wanted to be like his dad and wear a big belt round his waist with a brass buckle and have a hammer tucked in the back of his trousers!

One evening my mum and dad went to visit some friends in another street and Jack, myself, Noel, Tom and

Jean, were sitting on the floor by the fire and I was reading them a fairy story. Suddenly the wind blew down the chimney and blew a flame out into the room. The draperies round the fireplace caught alight and we all began to panic, except Noel who ordered us out into the street, throwing our coats out after us. "I'll let you know when it's safe to come in" he said

After a while he appeared at the street door, his face all black with soot. He had a seaside pail on his head with the handle under his chin, a piece of tarpaulin wrapped round his body and dad's big hobnail boots on. I said "Whatever are you dressed up like that for?" He shouted back "For protection. It's no good putting out a fire if you get burnt yourself. Now come on in and start cleaning up the kitchen. Jack you're the eldest, you start, Tom get a flannel and half fill a pail with hot water". "Where am I to get the hot water?" Tom asked. "Where do you think, out of the kettle of course, or do you think we are like the Romans? We don't have any hot springs like they built here." Jack exclaimed, "Romans? Who are the Romans? I've never heard of them." "Well I have" I said. "Just because Jack hasn't, he's not stupid." Noel took the pail from his head and shook hands with Jack. "Sorry old chap" he said. When everything was cleared up, if it hadn't been for the draperies burnt, nobody would have known what had happened.

When we were all sitting down again Jack said "Noel, tell us about the Romans, were they grown men?" "The Romans were soldiers in flaming armour" he explained. "They had shining helmets with eagles on them, on their heads. They invaded our island and stayed for hundreds of years." "Did they bring ladies with them?" Jack asked, and when Noel told us that yes, ladies did come too, Jack said "Could you draw me one of their dresses, then I'll make one, I'm a dress designer." "I'll tell you what I will do" said Noel, "I'll take you all to see the Roman Baths, only you'll have to walk, we'll call it a walking tour." Jean perked up, she had been quiet all along. "I'm not walking all that way. Unless I can go by train, I'm not coming."

Then Mum and Dad came in and bought us each a nice apple pie, so the Romans were soon forgotten. When I told my parents how Noel had taken charge of us and the fire, my dad said, prophetically, as it would eventually turn out, " Noel is going to be a very brave man one day."

★ ★ ★

One Easter Day my dad took us to see Westminster Abbey, Jack, myself, Noel Tom and Jean. We rode in a tram car from the Walworth Road to Westminster Bridge and then we walked half way over the bridge, stopping half way to eat our sandwiches. As we walked over the bridge we looked up to see 'Big Ben' and my dad told us that it was the biggest clock in the world.

When we went into Westminster Abbey my dad said "Take your caps off boys", so I took my hat off too. Then an Abbey Guide came up to my dad and said "Does this girl belong to you?" "Of course she does, she's my daughter." "Well, we don't allow females in the Abbey without a hat." I quickly put it on. "Kids" said the Guide, "no more sense than they were born with."

My dad walked us round and round the Abbey, telling us about everything until late into the afternoon, it seemed like hours and hours, until Jean said "I'm tired I want to go home. You carry me Dad, I'm not going to walk." Dad picked her up and said "We'd better start for home." Then we all said we were tired and hungry, so we walked to the tram stop. While we were walking to the tram stop Jack commented that all he could see in his head were dead men lying on marble slabs or standing up with cloaks round them. "Stone cold dead, and been like that for years. I shall be pleased to get home."

When the tram arrived we scrambled on. The conductor shouted "Full up inside, on top only", so my dad bundled us all up the stairs and at long last we were sitting in our seats. Then up came the conductor, "Fares please" he shouted and stood waiting while my dad fumbled in his pocket for some loose change... "Good Lord" my dad exclaimed. "My money has slipped through a hole in the lining of my trouser pocket. I haven't got a penny, no money at all. I've lost it." "Then you'll all have to get off, won't you" said the conductor. Pulling the cord as he spoke he stopped the tram car and we all had to scramble down the stairs and on to the pavement. "Well" said my dad, "there's only one thing for it, we'll have to walk home." "Walk?" exclaimed Jack, "All that way. I'm tired." "You're tired?" said Jean, "What do you think I am? I can't walk." "Well, we're all tired" I said, trying to calm things down. "Stop that silly crying Jean" Noel said to Jean and then turned to my dad, "This is a situation we must tackle. We can't stay here all night," so my dad picked up Jean and started walking. Noel said to Tom "Come on, let's hold hands and we can sing all the way home," and they started singing "There's a friend for little children above the bright blue sky."

Then it started to rain really hard, it simply poured down, and Tom shouted "I've lost my shoe, the button came off and it's fallen in the road. I think a bus just ran over it." "Jack and Kit" my dad called out "you give Tom a bandy chair." We continued to walk through the streets and not a further word was spoken until we arrived home drenched to our skins. My mother had already got hot water ready as she had guessed something like this had happened and we all had a hot bath and hot beautiful home made soup. As we were going upstairs to bed Noel looked over the banisters and said "Dad, when I'm older I think I will be a sewer official. I'd love to go down a sewer." Dad replied "You're better at putting out fires. Why not be a fireman?" Mother, tucking us up in bed, just said "Don't forget to say your prayers".

In June 1912 Keturah's eldest brother Harry married his sweetheart Bessie. Although Clara and Margaret were now married and Annie engaged, this was the eldest son's wedding, so John decided that they would have a formal photograph taken of the whole family, all ten of them, as a souvenir of this special occasion.

It was a lovely wedding. Margaret made all our clothes and the sun shone when we had our family photograph taken. Even now, after all the years gone by, each time I look at it, it still feels to me as if it was taken yesterday.

It is indeed a very special picture, of great significance to the end of Keturah's story, so a detailed description is both relevant and important. John, dressed in his wedding finery, sits proudly in the middle of the picture, his large, strong hands on his knees, and beside him is Charlotte, wearing an elegant white lace ruffled blouse. The four older girls sit proudly on either side of their parents. They are wearing their new gowns, unsmiling, their heads are held high and they are looking steadfastly at the camera. All the men and boys, apart from little Walter, wear smart jackets with carnations in their buttonholes, and the women have beautiful corsages pinned onto their dresses. Jean, Tom and Walter sit cross-legged at the front, Jean beribboned in a pretty dress, Tom with a starched white collar and five-year-old Walter in a white jumper. There are only two in the group who are smiling. Tom has a cheeky grin and Noel, already a handsome young man, gives a flashing smile.

This is the only photograph of the family together. No-one was to know that in just a few weeks' time this family would suffer a devastating blow from which it would never fully recover.

A family tragedy

*The 2ⁿᵈ Walworth Scout Troop; Tom and Noel say goodbye;
gale force winds; waiting for news; the shipwrecked sailor
returns; Charlotte and John live with their own traumas;
eight white coffins; the saddest day; a ray of sunshine.*

The following chapter must have been very difficult for
my aunt to write. It was always difficult for her to talk
about these distressing days, but to write about them in
considerable detail, 65 years afterwards, must have been
emotionally draining. No wonder she stopped writing at
the end of this chapter, she would have been exhausted.

I thought it important to make minimum changes
to this section of Keturah's writing. By doing so I hope
to have held on to the powerful feelings expressed in the
next few pages.

Noel and Tom belonged to the Walworth Scouts where the
Scoutmaster was Sidney Marsh, a 'Pay Master' in the navy.
He owned a boat, a former naval cutter,[15] he said it was,

15. A cutter is a very manoeuvrable, small, single-masted sailing boat, fore and aft rigged, with two or
more head sails and maybe a bowsprit. There are many different types of cutter which can be powered
by sail or oars. John Filmer, in his youth, would have sailed in a Naval Cutter, the lowest class of
classification, coming below the 'sloop of war' as an unrated vessel.

and often took the Scouts out on the Thames on a Saturday afternoon. The Scoutmaster knew about my dad's naval experience and asked him if he would help train the boys in seamanship, and my dad really enjoyed giving the boys lessons in splicing ropes and sewing sails. My sister Annie's young man, Len de Vulder, also helped Scoutmaster Marsh to train the Scouts in swimming, running and boxing.

It is now August 1912 and Scoutmaster Marsh is making plans to take his Scouts to camp at Leysdown on the Isle of Sheppey. He wanted the Scouts to go to camp in the cutter, so he asked my dad and Len if they would help him over the August Bank Holiday weekend. It was all arranged, Dad, Len and the Scouts would all go to Leysdown together in Scoutmaster Marsh's cutter. This was going to be a very fine trip.

★ ★ ★

On Saturday morning, August 3rd 1912, kitbags packed, Tom and Noel set off to walk to London Bridge where the cutter was moored. Mother, Jean, Walter and I stood on the door step and waved them goodbye until they were out of sight. Dad and Len joined them at London Bridge where the Scoutmaster and the rest of the Scouts were waiting. Annie waved them goodbye from the water's edge.

When I shut the door after saying goodbye to my brothers, I saw that my mother was crying. "I wish they were not going by sea" she said. "Oh, they'll be alright" I tried to reassure her, "Dad and Len are with them and they know a lot about the sea. "Yes, but Dad is not in charge of the cutter, Scoutmaster Marsh is the captain and his orders must be obeyed, otherwise there would be mutiny" she responded. When Annie came in she said everyone was happy when they sailed away. "I said to Noel 'you must look after Tom, don't let him wander anywhere alone'." My mother asked Annie "What did Noel say?" and she replied "he saluted me and said 'I will'."

★ ★ ★

On that Saturday night a gale blew up and at three o'clock in the morning mother came into my room. "Have you heard the wind? It's blowing gale - force, it's been like this for hours." I had heard it, but did not want to worry my mother, so I went downstairs and made a cup of tea. Then there was a loud bang as the chimney pot blew off. We stayed downstairs until daylight, and still the gale was blowing. After breakfast I tried to persuade my mother to rest upstairs, but she didn't want to. And still the gale was blowing. Just before lunch Walter and Jean came in to tell us that the roof had broken off the house next door. I could not persuade my mother to eat her lunch so I said "Sit in Dad's armchair and try to sleep" which she did, and she fell into a deep sleep. At exactly five minutes to two o'clock my mother woke suddenly, she stood up and said "Kit, it's all over, it's all over." "You've been dreaming" I said. Suddenly the wind dropped, the sun shone brilliantly and the sky was blue.

★ ★ ★

I made tea, but Mother was too exhausted to lift the cup, so I put it up to her mouth for her to drink, and then she seemed a little better as she looked out of the window at the sun. In the afternoon Jean, Walter, Mother and I played Snap until early evening when there was a knock on our street door. I opened the door and there stood the Vicar from St. John's Church, Walworth. I knew him pretty well because the Scouts used to go there for their services and Church Parades. He came into our sitting room and spoke to Mother. "Mrs Filmer, your sons are no more, but thank God you have your husband and your intended son-in-law. The cutter capsized at five minutes to two this afternoon." I looked over to where my mother was standing, she was deathly white and unable to speak. "She got caught in a squall and overturned," went on the Vicar. "I hear that nine Scouts are drowned, eight have been washed ashore and one is missing. I hear the coast guards were very quick on the scene although they had a long hard row. Your husband and Len will be home soon and I will stay with you until they come".

* * *

The news had soon got round for our street was crowded with people, newspaper reporters, policemen, parents of the other Scouts asking about their sons. Then my dad came home in a cab. All he wore was a sailor's flannel shirt and sailor's trousers and a pair of old carpet slippers, all given to him by the Leysdown coastguards. His feet were too swollen for him to be able to wear his boots and his hands, feet and face were blue, as he had been in the sea for a considerable time. As I opened the door my dad and all the newspaper reporters came in and the policemen had to hold the crowds back. I feel I cannot describe this, it all seemed like a bad dream. Then the doctor came to see my mum and dad, he gave them some sleeping pills and said they must both go to bed. Still crowds were hanging round the house so the policemen ordered them away.

* * *

The reporter from *The Daily Chronicle* wrote in poignant detail of the grief and anguish he had witnessed that evening:

All the sadness of Walworth seemed to centre on Sunday night round the little house near Dulwich Mission, where Mr Filmer, the only survivor who had yet returned home, was torn between grief at the loss of his sons, and sympathy with those anxious ones, who coming for news, had to be sent away sorrowing.

It was a pitiful scene in the little front parlour. Mrs Filmer was striving bravely to fight back her tears as she turned to comfort a neighbour who had been told that her son was drowned.

Once a big burly fellow, over six feet high, pushed through the crowd and came in at the open door. "My boy alright?" he asked in an eager husky whisper. "No mate, he's gone," replied Mr Filmer, and for a moment he forgot his own grief to put an arm, tender as a woman's, round his friend. It was as well that he did so because the giant flinched for a moment, then reeled and burst into tears.

White- faced women, some too stunned by the news to weep, filled the little room, eager for every scrap of news, as Mr Filmer told his story. Others knocked on the front door, and although there was no room for them, begged pitifully for tidings".

★ ★ ★

Later that evening I put Walter and Jean to bed and then sat on the couch until the early hours of the morning when my brothers and sisters came. I gave them some breakfast and they came back after work in the evening. My dad, Harry and Jack would have a lot to do arranging matters.

My mother got up and came downstairs and then we had another visit from the Vicar who said he now had a complete picture of the accident and thought that he was the right person to explain this to my mother. Mother, still in a state of shock, turned her head away and said she didn't want to hear, but the Vicar said "Mrs Filmer, you must listen to what I have to say, it will help you more later on than now." I persuaded Mother to listen and the Vicar told her all he knew about what had happened.

"The cutter capsized and your husband was thrown clear and went under. By his presence of mind he found a rope that was attached to the boat, and he pulled himself along to the upturned vessel. He called out to the Scouts who were swimming about close by him to help him right the boat, which they did and then told them to hang on to the boat. While your brave husband was lying across the middle of the boat he saw Noel and told him to hang on for his life. If it hadn't been for your husband's bravery it is likely all would have been lost. Your son Noel asked the Scout next to him if he had seen Tom, and he said he had seen Scoutmaster Marsh with Tom on his back, and then he saw a wave wash him off and he went under. Noel was heard to say "My brother's gone and I am going". He left hold of the boat and went under. Mrs Filmer, you have not only a brave husband, but a very brave son. You have a hard cross to bear, but God will give you the strength to bear it." The Vicar proved to be right, my mother did seem to be able to cope better.

My father spoke very little. He told the press all he knew and consoled the parents who had lost their sons, but at home he was grief stricken. To see this man of the sea, a tough, rugged sailor who had sailed the world in windjammers, to see this man cry... I felt sure he would never be the same again. All he kept saying was "They would have all gone if I had not righted the boat, but my sons... Is there a God?" Poor Dad.

We were concerned for my mother's health too. She spoke very little to Dad or to the rest of the family, but told me that I was her mainstay. She said to me "If it wasn't for you Kit, I would not survive." Dearest mother, she and Dad had struggled so hard to look after us, always caring for others, a Godly lady.

* * *

A few days later eight white coffins covered with Union Jacks came to Cherry Orchard Pier. One coffin had a wreath on it with a card which said "Noel Filmer – for his bravery. From the Coastguards. He gave his life for his brother when he knew his brother was lost to the sea." The coffins were taken in procession through Rotherhithe and through the streets of Walworth, until they reached St John's Church, where they would lie in state until the funeral day. And still the other poor Scout had not been found; it was complete agony to see his parents.

The eight white coffins were now lying in state for the Walworth people to come to pray, but others came too, from far and wide, to pray for the Scouts, and for the boy who was still to be found. Twice a day my parents went to the church to be close to the coffins. It was so wonderfully sad to go into the church, the silence sometimes broken by sobs of the grief stricken, as the thousands of people walked quietly round the Godly white coffins of those innocent young Scouts. The prayers of the Vicar, and of the other clergymen who came to pray, must have been a great solace to the parents of the lost Scouts.

When I thought of Noel, I knew that he would have done this brave act. Noel was always brave.

The day before the funeral we went to the church privately to say farewell, as the funeral was to be a public one. I shall never forget the scene in the church and my poor mum and dad. I dreaded the morrow. How could my poor mum stand up to it? There was one consolation, Harry would look after Mum. He was a great son, staunch and sound. I loved him, I loved them all.

★ ★ ★

After the service the long funeral procession started from

St John's Church about midday. Crowds were lining both sides of the route. Shops had been closed for the day and from their crowded windows people were looking. Each family had its own horse and carriage and an open carriage for its flowers and wreaths. Lieutenant General Baden Powell had sent beautiful floral tributes of eight life buoys made of white and purple asters, one for each Scout. Slowly the procession moved through the streets until it came to Nunhead Cemetery[16], where again there were hundreds of people lining the paths to the open grave. The service was read, the Last Post sounded and the mourners walked sadly back to their carriages. It would have taken the strongest nerve not to have been broken.

Back home, when my elder brothers and sisters had left and there remained just Mum, Dad, Jean, Walter and myself, our house was silenced. My mother and father sat down, overwhelmed with sadness. I went into the sitting room and noticed that someone had locked the piano. No more would we hear Noel play their Scout songs while Tom sang them. Walter asked me if he could go and see his friend; poor little chap, he was not old enough to understand. My mother began crying and my poor dad was not able to console her. I thought to myself 'God, how am I going to be able to get through this first evening?' I did not know and I wished I could escape. I had not slept for a week. Then there was a knock at the door.

I thought 'That will be Walter wanting to come in', but to my great surprise there were three of the Browning

16. Nunhead Cemetery is one of seven Victorian cemeteries to be established in a ring around the outskirts of London. Nunhead was consecrated in 1840. It contains examples of magnificent monuments to eminent citizens of the day as well as small simple headstones. It is a place of natural beauty, its avenues reminiscent of country lanes from bygone days.

Club boys, come to pay their respects to my parents. My eyes filled with tears and I didn't have a handkerchief so the auburn-haired young man took his handkerchief from the top pocket of his jacket and said to me "It's not for keeps you know." I smiled and thanked him.

To my great surprise my parents invited them in and I made tea and gave them cakes which were already on the table. To see a smile on their faces was surely something wonderful. Then they asked my dad if they would like to be taken to a Garden Fete the next week, which they were getting up to enable the poor children to have an outing. My mum and dad said they would love to go – surely this visit was heaven sent!

After the Garden Fete, the Browning Boys, as they were known, although they were really young men, came round once a week to see my parents, and always the auburn-haired young man came too. Later on he asked my father if he could take me to see a 'Musical', and the end of this story is that my dad said that he would make a jolly good son-in-law, and that led to fifty-seven years of my very happy marriage.

Keturah's story abruptly ends here, but, after all that dreadful sadness, at least it finishes on a note of optimism. She leaves her reader with no hint of how the rest of the family subsequently coped with the loss of their sons and brothers, in particular John and Charlotte. I will attempt to do this in the final chapter of this book.

From a family perspective the deaths of Noel and

Tom were a cruel family tragedy, but to the wider world, the loss of all nine Scouts was a national event and became known as the Leysdown Tragedy. The following chapter will attempt to deal with this broader perspective from a well-documented historical viewpoint.

The Leysdown tragedy in retrospect

THE STORY OF THE TRAGEDY

It was just five years earlier that Lieutenant General Robert Baden-Powell had organised an experimental camp for a group of both privileged and underprivileged boys on Brownsea Island in Poole Harbour. Such was the success of this venture that the concept of Scouting spread rapidly across the country. Boys in their thousands were themselves setting up troops and finding their own leaders. Scouting, offering out-door, challenging activities which would help to encourage self-reliance and good citizenship, had obviously struck a chord in the nation's youth.

In the early days of the Scout Movement there was no differentiation between land and water-based Scouting. Baden-Powell based his original ideas about the movement on his own boyhood memories and his love of the open air. He wrote "Sea Scouting is not necessarily a scheme for training a boy as a ready-made sailor with a view to going to sea, but rather to teach him, by means which attract him, to be a handy, quick and disciplined man, able to look after himself and others in danger. Boat handling, swimming and life saving in the water can be taught to inland troops just as well as those belonging to the coast."

★ ★ ★

The 2nd Walworth Scout Troop (Dulwich Mission) was formed at St John's Church in Larcom Street in around 1910. The Scoutmaster, Sidney Marsh, had already bought himself a cutter and soon began to take the Scouts out on the river, training his boys in seamanship. After the Leysdown accident the Scout Headquarters' records noted "There can be no doubt about the boys' fitness to sail to Leysdown, for though they were not Sea Scouts, under Scoutmaster Marsh, the 2nd Walworth had attained a high standard of seamanship and all the boys had learned to swim".

Sidney Marsh, the Scoutmaster of the 2nd Walworth Troop, was an ex-Dulwich College boy and a licensed lay reader attached to the Dulwich College Mission. For years there were many such missions operating in southeast London, all playing major roles in social work amongst local underprivileged families. Marsh was described as a charismatic young man, working by day in the City of London, and returning in the evening to Walworth, where he rented two rooms in one of the poorest quarters of the area. He believed that he owed a debt to society and that it was his Christian duty to help deprived families, and this he did with enormous enthusiasm. The newly-formed Boy Scouts' Association gave him additional opportunities to offer to the 'slum kids' of Walworth challenge and adventure in the fresh air whenever possible.

Having had a successful two-week camp at Leysdown in 1911, Sidney Marsh would have been quite confident about repeating the adventure in 1912, and one can imagine the Scouts' mounting excitement as they prepared themselves for their journey down the Thames. There was no reason not to believe that the 1912 expedition would be a great experience for all involved.

★ ★ ★

It was 5 pm when the Walworth Troop set off from London Bridge on their journey to Leysdown. Having said goodbye to family and friends they were ready to go. The Scouts had been well trained, so boots, blankets and kitbags were carefully stowed away before making ready to row into the centre of the river. The boys rowed the first mile and a half to Tower Bridge, but the current was with them so it was not hard work; once past the bridge the oars were stowed, the mast stepped and the sails hoisted. They sailed down the busy river under an overcast sky but by the time they got to Erith at 9 pm it was raining slightly, so Scoutmaster Marsh decided to go alongside for the night.

The Scouts would not have much rest that night.

Sleeping on the bottom of the boat covered only by a blanket and the sails would have been pretty uncomfortable, so at around 4 am, with not much more than a drink of water, they set off on the final part of the journey. The wind was picking up as they sailed by Gravesend, so Scoutmaster Marsh put his three strongest Scouts on the sails. Soon the river turned east and began to broaden into the Thames estuary, by now almost a mile wide.

All was going well as they sailed across the mouth of the River Medway in a freshening breeze, but as they got closer to Leysdown, Scoutmaster Marsh became aware of a depression approaching from the south-west. He now had to make a decision: furl the sails, or make full speed to land to get the boys into camp where hot food would be waiting.

The Leysdown Coastguards were expecting the Scouts aboard their cutter and it had been agreed that a look-out would be posted to receive the signal from the cutter as she rounded Warden Point. Warden Point remains a dangerous area for the navigation of small boats; to the southwest the shelter of high cliffs off Sheppey fall away suddenly, and the wind diverts and is swept on to the open sea, causing eddies and whirlpools. At approximately 1.30 pm the look-out sighted the cutter and signalled to Scoutmaster Marsh, who then gave the order to 'go about'. Having readjusted the sails and with Marsh at the helm, the cutter headed straight for the shore when there was a sudden change in the wind direction and abreast Warden Point a violent rainsquall struck the cutter.

Marsh put the helm over and snatched the mainsheet from the Scout and the cutter came up a little then heeled over, filling with water and tipping the Scouts on the lee side into the water. The cutter then righted itself before capsizing again and John Filmer, who was sitting on the side of the boat, was flung into the water. As he came up, he found himself tangled up in ropes and under the mainsail which was by now flat on the water. Although held down by his heavy coat he managed to catch hold of a rope and pull himself along in the water. By now the cutter had shaken most of the Scouts into the sea. Some were swept away, while others held on to the side of the boat.

With a heavy swell running, all those in the water were soon suffering from exhaustion. Marsh made valiant efforts to save his boys, nearly drowning himself. Briefly he had Tom on his back and tried to swim with him to the upturned boat, but a wave knocked him off. John called out "Oh sir, look after my son Tom". Noel turned to the Scout next him asking if he had seen his brother and the Scout told him he had seen Tom washed off the Scoutmaster's back. Noel's brave reply was "Is my brother gone? And I am going." He let go of the boat and dived under the waves.

Eight Scouts were drowned that day, as well as a young lad from the training ship *Arethusa*.

Meanwhile the coastguards had witnessed the

capsize, and at a risk to their own lives launched their lifeboat with four coastguards as crew. They rowed two miles through heavy seas and rescued five adults and sixteen Scouts, who had all been in the water for over half an hour and were exhausted. As the survivors were revived they were taken into the homes of the coastguards, where they were cared for until they regained their strength.

The destroyer HMS *Actean* and the government tug *Security* were despatched to locate the cutter and search for bodies. The capsized boat was picked up later on the oyster grounds at Whitstable along with the dinghy she was towing, which still contained various articles of clothing and John Filmer's gold watch. It had stopped at five minutes to two.

When interviewed by the press next morning Scoutmaster Marsh said "I have lived in Walworth for five years in order to be right amongst my boys. They are all working class boys and we had all been looking forward to this holiday trip. The cutter was quite seaworthy, and nothing could have averted the disaster when the squall came. But it is all too horrible for me to talk about. I am heart-sick and weary."

Early that next morning eight bodies had been sighted lying on the sand and were brought to shore by the coastguards. One of them said "All of them looked so peaceful, as though death had been easy and painless. We carried them on our shoulders. They were so light. I hope I never go through such a time again". The body of the ninth drowned Scout was recovered some days later in Margate.

One of the Scouts who died, Patrol Leader William Beckham, had two brothers in the boat who were saved. At the inquest his mother said she would be eternally grateful to Scoutmaster Marsh for saving the lives of her other two sons, John and Edward. David Beckham, the former England footballer, is the great-grandson of Edward.

★ ★ ★

On August 7th, before the inquest was held, each body had to be formally identified, and it was Harry, John and Charlotte's eldest child, who undertook this difficult task on behalf of his parents. During the inquest into the cause of death, Scoutmaster Marsh explained that the squall caught the cutter when she was on starboard tack and was not able to withstand the shock of the impact. Evidence showed that the adults and Scouts were all appropriately trained and prepared and that the accident was due to no fault of seamanship, but was attributed to a squall from the land striking the boat.

Today the Scout Association has stringent rules in place and highly-qualified advisers appointed to ensure that the adults in charge of such an activity are trained and assessed to a high standard; they also approve equipment and plans for such a potentially dangerous venture, but in 1912 it was just Scoutmaster Marsh who accepted that responsibility. The Coroner recorded a verdict of 'accidentally drowned' and Sidney Marsh was commended for his bravery.

★ ★ ★

On Friday August 8th the bodies of the eight boys in their white coffins were brought back to London in a manner more often associated with royalty. At that time Winston Churchill was First Lord of the Admiralty. Maybe not only to show his approval of Baden Powell's achievements in setting up the Boy Scout Association but to show his sympathy with the Walworth Scouts and their Leaders, he arranged for a destroyer, *HMS Fervant*, to bring them home.

Here is another quotation from a newspaper, this time *The Sheerness Times*, written in the style of the period, the writer interpreting the sadness of the occasion with great eloquence.

Few of those who assembled on the beach at Leysdown to witness the removal of the bodies at the conclusion of the inquest, will ever forget the solemn and impressive scene. The Sheppey Boy Scouts lined the route to the beach, standing with bowed heads and with both hands clutching their staves.

The bodies, each enclosed in coffins of elm painted white with gilt facings, were then brought down to the beach. On either side of the coffins the remaining Scouts from the 2nd Walworth Troop formed an escort, and immediately behind them came Scoutmaster Marsh and the relatives of the dead Scouts. The white ensign flying above the Coastguard Station had been lowered to half-mast and HMS Fervant and all boats down at the shore also dipped their ensigns at the given signal. The Scoutmasters gave the Scout's salute as the bodies were borne on their way. By twos the coffins were placed in waiting boats and covered with a naval ensign, then pulled out to sea by the strong arms of sailors whose oars were muffled.

There was no music, no blare of bugle or beat of drum, all was done in silence which rendered the sad spectacle the more impressive.

By seven o'clock the last of the bodies had been transferred to the deck of HMS Fervant, and as the shadows of eventide were spreading across the sea, the warship stole silently away and passed out of sight round Warden Pont on its passage up the Thames. The Thames, it seemed, lay still to await them, cranes ceased to rattle, port boatmen lay on their oars, all ships flew their flags at half mast.

The *Fervant* had been painted black from her waterline from stem to stern, even her life belts were painted black, so she must have looked a sombre sight as she moored at Cherry Garden Pier the next morning. There was a naval guard of honour for the disembarkation of the bodies of the Scouts. The guard presented arms and then, one by one, the coffins were carried ashore by the sailors to the waiting hearses. The bodies of Noel and Tom were conveyed in the same hearse.

On arrival at St John's Church, Walworth, the coffins were carried in and laid at the foot of the altar, each covered with a Union Jack and with wreaths from family and friends placed on them. Scouts stood in front of each coffin, heads bowed, and they remained there throughout the night, fresh contingents of Scouts arriving to take their turn in watching over the dead boys. Across the country prayers were said for the Scouts. This was indeed a time of national mourning.

* * *

The church remained open throughout Saturday August 9th for those who wished to pay their respects. No one could have anticipated the vast numbers who would throng to Walworth that day; it is said that more than 100,000 people passed through the church. *The Daily Express* reported:

It was like a dream, this lily-scented church and the endless procession of men and women, who came and went like phantom figures. Rich and poor, mothers who could not keep back their tears, men with grave faces and children numb with awe, all paid their tribute.

* * *

On the day of the funeral South London came to a halt. From early morning the people had formed up in silence, eight deep in some places, and despite drenching rain there were more than a million people lining the streets as the cortege went by. Boy Scouts, linked together by their staves, formed a barrier which no one crossed. The storm passed with the funeral service and as the procession lined up outside the church the sun shone brightly. Traffic had been diverted from local roads and the busy streets were lulled into silence as the hearses passed by. The procession, a mile long, took nearly an hour to reach the cemetery. An anonymous donor had given a plot of land in South London's most expensive cemetery, Nunhead, so that the Scouts could be buried together. Few members of royalty or statesmen have ever been given such an honour as that given to those eight Scouts. The multitude which witnessed that dramatic day saw what can only be described as a state funeral.

★ ★ ★

Even before the funeral, the Boy Scouts' Association had endorsed a memorial fund which had been set up by *The Daily Express* called 'A fund for 1,000,000 pennies'. Money poured in from across the world, from the rich and from the poor. What follows are extracts from just a few letters from those sending donations:

Delighted to send five pounds and so show appreciation of what is probably the finest movement in our time.

Signed. Waldorf
Astor, Cliveden

Dear Sir, I enclose 12 pennies towards the memorial for my brother. I felt I ought to send more than one penny, as if I had not had a sore throat, I might have been one of them .

Yours truly
J. H. Crook

Dear Mr Express, I am sending you five shillings for the memorial for the poor boys. That is all I have in my bank. Daddy says I would be a Scout if I was old enough, but I am a little girl[17].

From Marjorie

Two years later a magnificent memorial was erected over the graves where the boys had been buried. Commissioned by *The Daily Express*, designed by Sir Giles Gilbert Scott RA and sculpted by Miss Lillie Reed, it soon became known as 'The Mourning Scout'. The sculpture was a life-sized bronze of a Scout standing, head bowed and holding his stave. There was careful attention to detail; the shirt sleeves were rolled up, as Baden-Powell had encouraged Scouts to be ever ready to help out, and for neatness, the sleeves were rolled up on the inside. The whole monument was eight feet high, one of the finest in the cemetery, and people came in their hundreds over the years just to see the Boy Scouts' grave.

Although initially the memorial was cleaned and maintained by local Scouts, over the years, and particularly during and after the Second World War, the memorial, and indeed the whole cemetery, began to fall into disrepair. By 1969, Nunhead Cemetery was in such a run-down state that the owners were unable to cope

17. It was not until 1991 that girls were finally entitled to be Scouts. It is now mandatory that all Scout Groups offer Scouting to girls as well as to boys

with the maintenance. The cemetery was regularly vandalised and one night the unbelievable happened. The statue was sawn off at the ankles and stolen, no doubt sold on for scrap, the estimated value being £40. No evidence of the statue has ever been found, but the original brass plaque did turn up in a scrap yard in nearby Charlton in 1997 and now rests in the archives of the Scout Association.

Slowly the memorial to the boys disintegrated into a pile of rubble. Many people did not even know of its original existence, but there were still older locals and Scout Leaders who did remember and who thought it wrong that there was nothing to mark the boys' grave, so they suggested raising money to rectify this.

There is fortunately a happy ending to this story of desecration, for in 1991 the Friends of Nunhead Cemetery were able to arrange for a replacement memorial to be put on the site of the original one. The new memorial, generously funded by a local monumental mason and funeral director, was in the form of a white marble book and engraved with the names of all the lost Scouts, the Scout emblem and the 'Gone Home' sign.

In April 1992, under grey skies and a steady downpour, just as at the Boy Scouts' funeral service eighty years before, a Scout bugler from Dulwich College, Scoutmaster Marsh's old school, played the Last Post as the new monument was formally consecrated. The boys who perished in the Leysdown Tragedy are once again publicly remembered.

More recently, on August 12th 2012 the Friends of Nunhead Cemetery organised a commemorative ceremony and the dedication of a centenary memorial in memory of 'Walworth's Lost Boys'.

Consequences

Keturah's memoirs close fairly abruptly once she has described the days following the funeral, and I have only vague and disconnected aural records of what happened to the rest of the family after the tragedy. However I thought it was important to try to draw some threads together before ending this book, and this is what I have done, firstly by just thinking about the family and then wondering about what might have happened as all the family members began to move on with the rest of their lives.

The days, weeks and months following the loss of Tom and Noel must have been almost unbearable for both John and Charlotte, heartbroken, crushed and lost in their own misery as they were. Living with them at this time was Keturah, doing her best to look after her mother and the two younger children, Jean aged ten and Walter five. The gaping hole left by the two boys would have been ever present and impossible to fill. A crisis such as John and Charlotte faced was a novel situation and there would have been no guidance for them on how to cope. The days of producing babies were now over. What, if anything, could or would hold them together?

It is generally accepted that men and women express their emotions very differently and will work through the pain of bereavement in their own ways, so friction is bound to occur and there can be many misunderstandings at this fragile time. Men, following maybe a time of tears and sadness, will probably want to get back to work, do something concrete, anything to keep the distress at bay, whilst women tend to cry more and longer and need time to retell their stories to people who will listen and understand. The man may feel that the woman has become stuck in her grief, that she no longer has any time for him. The woman may think that the man does not care, because he is trying to move on with his life. It is entirely possible for couples to work their way together through the period of grief after the death of their child, but for this to happen, so that they can emerge with their relationship still intact at the end of their period of mourning, close communication and mutual understanding and respect will be required. Much will also depend on the quality of their previous relationship.

John and Charlotte had been together for nearly thirty years when Noel and Tom died. They had already lost four children, but had mutually supported each other through the lean years when John had often been out of work and there was little money to provide a basic standard of living for their large family. Charlotte, as well as being a dutiful wife and mother, had always worked long hours in the laundry to help supplement the family income. It appears that their relationship had been, to date, robust enough to hold the family together, so would it be able to survive this unexpected and terrible loss of two further children?

John, a strong, practical man, would have probably got back to work as quickly as possible after the funeral. He would not have wanted to stay in the house listening to the quiet weeping of his distraught wife, and of course he had to find ways of living not only with his own vivid memories of the accident at sea, but also with the anguish and guilt that he had survived and the fact that his sons had been lost to the sea. His boys were gone and could not be replaced, John would have seen himself as to blame and his natural sadness could well have turned into depression. Today he would have been offered support and counselling; he was probably suffering from what we now call post-traumatic stress disorder for a period of time, but no one knew about that in 1912. You were just supposed to 'get over it'.

Charlotte was not a well woman when Noel and Tom were drowned. She was slowly regaining her strength after suffering a heart attack and was being cared for by Keturah, but the loss of her sons set her back again, and from then until her death in 1936, Charlotte was a semi-invalid.

Two years later came the outbreak of the First World War. Harry and Jack joined up straight away and in 1915 so did John, taking ten years off his age in order to be accepted for military service. All three men survived, despite having been wounded and spending time in hospital. John's military records indicate that he joined the Royal Engineers 700th Labour Company and was promoted from Lance Corporal to Corporal before being admitted to hospital in 1917.

It was around this time that John made a decision that would once again upset the equilibrium of the family. He decided to walk away from his family and move to Middleton near Manchester to set up a new life with another woman, and he was not seen again by any family member for about twenty years.[18] Apparently he wrote to one or two family members to explain why he had done this, but gave no address, so from then on for the next twenty years he was basically out of contact with everyone. From a copy of a letter I have which John wrote to Harry some ten years later it looks as if he had settled happily into his new life, writing about a dog, about building a greenhouse and visits to the library. The woman John lived with had a son, but it is not known if this was John's child or the child of a former partner. However, at the outbreak of the Second World War this son, now a young man, joined the RAF and was sadly killed in 1940, maybe during the Battle of Britain. John wrote to Harry of his sadness at losing this boy, saying poignantly, "You never know how much you miss someone till they are gone, do you?"

---

18. John was not the first Filmer to move north to Manchester. Around 1879 one George Budds Filmer, great-great uncle of our John, moved there from his Newnham home in Kent, to set up home with his new wife. This was at the time when John Filmer was sailing the high seas as a teenager.

Why did John choose to leave his loyal wife and beloved children? We shall never know, but it could be that Charlotte, overwhelmed with her own feelings, was no longer able to give him the support and comfort he needed. Perhaps they both secretly wondered if it would have been better if John had died along with his boys. All conjecture. What I have now come to believe is that for the last twenty years of his life John was able to find someone with whom he could live comfortably, someone who could help him manage the never-ending pain of the loss of his sons. For him there had been some light at the end of a long, dark tunnel.

It was in 1936, the year that Charlotte died, that John, now aged seventy-seven, travelled south to try to reconnect with his family. My cousins Tom and Beryl answered the knock at their door and there stood a strange old man. They called their mother, Keturah, who, instantly recognizing her dear old dad, said "Is it you, or is it a ghost?" How many of John's children wished to meet their father again is not known, but Keturah, always a forgiving lady, was pleased to welcome him into her home on annual visits until his death in 1943.

Charlotte, with much support from Keturah, did her best to bring up Jean and Walter, but it cannot have been easy for any of them, most of all for young Walter, whose dad had abandoned him when he was just ten years old. Once Jean had left home Charlotte gave up her own home and she and Walter lived with Keturah until Walter married in 1930.

★ ★ ★

The one member of this large family I really knew and cared about, and who cared about me and my family, was Keturah, and because she and Walter had such a very special relationship, I have decided to keep them together for this part of the story. For much of Walter's life Keturah was more than a big sister; she was almost a mother, and always a friend. For well over half Walter's life until his marriage when he was twenty-three, much as he loved his mother, Keturah would have been central to his life. Later on, during and after the Second World War, Keturah and her husband Will again offered sanctuary to Walter for over ten years, whilst his own family lived in a safer environment in rural Wiltshire. Keturah's son, Walter's nephew, Thompson, remembers those years very well; he always enjoyed Walter's company and said he thought of him more as a big brother than an uncle.

In the period leading up to the loss of Noel and Tom, Keturah makes several references to "the Browning boys, particularly the one with the auburn hair." At this time she was sixteen going on seventeen and very aware that the one with the auburn hair was popular with all the girls! Would she stand a chance? My guess is that she and Will started to become closer following the boys' deaths; the lads' visits to her home would have provided a golden opportunity for the two of them to fall in love. They married three years later.

Walter would have been too young to remember much about Noel and Tom, but at ten he was certainly old enough to remember his father and to wonder where he was and why he hadn't come home once the war was over. My father never told me anything about his understanding of his own father's departure; families close ranks in these situations, maybe he had to just work it out for himself. For many years into his adult life Walter remained very angry with his father for leaving his frail mother and, most importantly, for abandoning him. When John returned to Keturah's house in 1937 Walter refused to see him and would not have his name mentioned in our house.

Years later, when he himself was an old man, Walter did once tell me, with tears in his eyes, how well he remembered his father and how he used to love it when he came home from work each evening. It is fully understandable that Walter would find it difficult to forgive the dad he trusted to always be there for him.

So how did Walter get on as a young lad? We know he did well at school, becoming Head Boy at King and Queen Street Boys' School and receiving prizes for excellent attainment. He also joined the 2nd Walworth Scout Troop, where Sidney Marsh was still Scoutmaster. Scouting was very important to Walter: he spoke very highly of his Scoutmaster, saying that he owed him a huge debt of gratitude for helping him establish his own beliefs, standards and values. Walter never became a First Class Scout because he was unable to pass one part of the swimmer's badge test. In order to pass this test he had to dive to the bottom of the pool to retrieve an object, and this he was never able to do. I have sometimes wondered if there could be any subconscious connection between his fear of being under the water and his own understanding of what had happened to his brothers.

When Walter left school at fourteen he was helped by his mother's family, who were in the printing trade, to obtain a seven-year apprenticeship as a vellum binder, at the end of which period he obtained a first-class certificate. My sister and I both have many examples of his high level of skill and craftsmanship, not only in book-binding, but in creating many beautiful leather objects embossed with gold-tooling.

Walter was just seventeen when he was approached by his two nephews, Noel and Len, who were Wolf Cubs. Their Cub Mistress was looking for more people to help run the Pack, and they wondered if Uncle Walter, now a Rover Scout, would go along and lend a hand. Walter did indeed help the Pack and slowly, over a period of seven years, got to know and eventually fall in love with the Cub Mistress, Cissie Adams, a woman thirteen years his senior and a year older than his sister Keturah. Cissie was of the generation which had lost so many young men to the Great War and she had so far dedicated her life to helping her mother bring up the younger children. She had also become a most accomplished pianist and organist. Cissie, who had grown up in a village on the North Downs of Kent, was well-read, an intelligent and articulate lady, and she enjoyed introducing Walter to the delights of literature, music and art and accompanied him on the piano when he sang.

Both families were much concerned when Cissie and Walter announced their intention to marry. Not only was there the obvious age difference, but they came from such different backgrounds, one a countrywoman, the other from an inner city area. However, those who had opposed their wish to marry need not have worried, for the marriage lasted 53 years. Cissie and Walter had two daughters, and despite an acute shortage of money for many years and an eleven-year separation during and after the Second World War, they found their own way of holding their marriage together.

When Keturah, now in her eighties, came to live in Buckinghamshire, her daughter Beryl used to drive her over to Oxfordshire to spend time with 'Walt', her baby brother. They would sit and reminisce about their childhood, but sometimes things would get quite heated, especially when they started talking about their father. Walter remained angry with his father, but Keturah still had loving memories of him and had obviously forgiven him. They never did agree.

When she was an old lady Cissie became muddled and sometimes quite difficult, but Walter lovingly cared for her throughout and was devastated when she died. He was still very young at heart and could perhaps have had further years to enjoy life, pursue his bookbinding activities and see more of his grandchildren, but losing Cissie was too much. He did not want to live without her and he died some fifteen months later in 1985.

★ ★ ★

This next section will be very short, something like a blurred photograph, as I have no Keturah to guide me and little relevant knowledge about John and Charlotte's other children. With such a large and extended family, it was never going to be easy for the siblings and their children to stay in close touch with each other, particularly after John left the family. Harry was twenty-one when my father, Walter, was born. He and Bessie had a long and happy marriage, they had three children, the second being Len, our family historian[19]. I met Harry once when I was about ten and remember him as very like the wedding photograph of my grandfather.

Annie, the second oldest child, did come into my life when I was about eleven. She and her husband Len had

19. Len Filmer, author of *Seven Generations of a Kent Family*, published by the Research Publishing Company in 1975.

lived in India for many years returning to England at the time of Partition[20] in 1947. Annie and Len lived in Ashtead in Surrey, which was close to where I lived, so we saw quite a lot of them. I remember them as kind and generous people who gave my sister and me presents and sometimes money.

I never met Margaret and Clara and know little about their lives, but Jack I met once. He never fulfilled his dreams of becoming a dress designer, although for a while he was employed as a clerk for a milliner. For most of his working life Jack worked for London Transport, firstly as a bus conductor and later as an inspector. At our only brief meeting, when I was about nine, he was wearing his inspector's uniform with a smart peaked cap.

Jean married a horse-racing jockey, and they had three children who all emigrated to Australia. When she was an elderly lady and a widow, Jean too moved to Australia where she lived out her final years. I have fifteen Filmer cousins, but have only met seven of them.

Harry's second son, Len, did become more closely involved with our family as he got older. Len was the family historian who, in his retirement, spent many years undertaking detailed research into past generations of the Filmer family. No internet to help you along with your research in those days, just hard

---

20. Partition – August 1947, when the Indian Independence Act set forth the details of the partition of India on the basis of religious demographics, and the new Islamic country of Pakistan came into being. This was a very difficult and dangerous time and many British citizens who had worked for years in India, decided that it was safer to return to the United Kingdom..

work letter-writing, studying parish records in the local library and visiting churchyards! It is to Len's work I have regularly referred whilst writing this book. When my parents celebrated their Golden Wedding in 1980, it was Len Filmer who gave an amusing speech and proposed a toast to his Aunt Cissie and very young Uncle Walter.

★ ★ ★

Although Sidney Marsh was not a family member, he did have an important influence on the lives of John, Noel, Tom and Walter through their involvement in Scouting, so this seems an appropriate place to make a final reference to him.

During World War I Sidney served with distinction as a Commander in the Royal Naval Reserve. He returned to Walworth in 1918, continuing with his life of care and support to the people of Walworth. My father, now fatherless, was both a Scout and a Rover Scout in the 2nd Walworth Troop until 1923 and told me many times how much he owed to Sidney Marsh.

There is little known about the rest of Sidney Marsh's life apart from a record indicating that in the early 1940s he was making arrangements to open his Camberwell house to be used as a carpentry workshop to instruct local Scouts.

The following quotation by the Rev. Everard Digby, the vicar of St Paul's, Covent Garden, spoken soon after the Leysdown tragedy, seems to sum up Scoutmaster Marsh's character and attitude to life.

"Marsh is a most capable man. That this disaster should have happened while he was in charge is the very worst luck. He is a splendid fellow and the sacrifices he makes for his boys are numberless. In town he is worshipped by the boys. Walworth swears by him, and with good reason. He is father, mother and everything else to them. He looks after their character, their training, in fact their whole lives. He is making real clean, self-respecting men out of them".

Walter, my father, many times echoed those sentiments. "Good old Marshie", he used to say, his eyes brimming with tears, "he showed me the right way to live, I might have gone under without him."

Reflections

Of the fourteen children born to John and Charlotte Filmer, eight survived into adulthood and between them those eight children produced eighteen of their own. There were only three men to carry forward the Filmer surname, Harry, Jack and Walter; Jack and Walter had daughters, but Harry and Bessie did produce two sons, Noel and Leonard, as well as a daughter, Ethel. In the next generation Noel had two daughters, but Leonard kept his branch of the Filmer name alive by having two sons, John and Andrew, as well as a daughter, Annette. John had two daughters, so it was just up to the youngest son, Andrew, to father a son, which he has successfully done, along with a daughter, Harriet. So now there is only one remaining male Filmer directly related to John and Charlotte, and that is Rufus Filmer, twenty-five years old at the time of writing. Time will tell if this line of the Filmer family will continue for another generation.

In modern times there is an increasing tendency for couples not to formalise their union, so following the male line is maybe not going to be as important as it was formerly. Perhaps in the future another family historian will follow the female (matrilineal) line[21] from Charlotte, her daughters and grand daughters. There's a challenge!

As a young child I grew up believing that all children had just one grandparent; in my case, I had just my 'gran'. My maternal grandfather had died when I was three and I barely remember him. My Filmer grandparents I never met, nor were they often spoken of, as John Filmer had absented himself from the family long before my parents were married and Charlotte died before I was born. I was thus hardly aware that I actually did have two Filmer grandparents, because if my father did ever refer to either of them, it would be always as 'my mother' or 'my father', never as 'your granny', or 'your grandpa'.

When I began to write this book I had not anticipated how the experience would also become a personal journey for me as I slowly began to discover that at last I was getting to know my Filmer grandparents and to think of them for the first time as Granny and Grandpa, which did feel rather strange at my age!

Grandpa John reminds me so much of my own father, Walter. They were alike not only in looks (short and bald), but in personality, devoted to their families, cheerful and outgoing, sporty and with a love for singing and dancing. John had a strong baritone voice, which

21. One tiny piece of our DNA, mitochondrial DNA, is inherited only down the female line. It would therefore be possible to follow the female line from Charlotte through her daughters, Margaret, Clara, Annie, Keturah and Jean, then on through their daughters, grand daughters and great grand daughters.

my father inherited. During the Second World War Walter used to take part in local concerts and became known as 'the barking baritone', and he is still remembered in my Oxfordshire village as the old man who used to ride his bicycle round the lanes singing at the top of his voice! When writing about the day when John and some of the children walked home from their visit to Westminster Abbey, I was reminded of a similar occasion when my father, sister and I missed the last bus home and had to walk five miles through the freezing Wiltshire countryside during the winter of 1947. What did we do? We sang all the way home!

Granny Charlotte has been an inspiration to me – what a wise, strong person, a woman of her times, worn out in mid-life, but ever thoughtful and courteous. My cousin, Len Filmer (23 years my senior), had clear memories of our grandmother; his family used to visit her when he was a child and he described her as a sweet lady who made the most delicious lemonade. I'm sure she would have been a wonderful grandparent and I am sad that I never knew her.

Although we were separated for eleven years through circumstances of war, I was able to enjoy some five teenage years with my father, Walter, when we moved to Surrey in 1951 and our family was finally reunited. We were the best of pals, but I was always aware that there were parts of his life that he obviously felt passionately about, but of which I knew little. Now I can understand why. The years after the deaths of Noel and Tom must have been confused and troubling for a young boy. Each family member had to find their own way through their grief; voices would have been hushed and there were matters talked about that were not suitable for a small boy's ears. When John, his father, left the family, young Walter was abandoned to an all-female world of big sisters and a sick mother – not the ideal environment for a young man growing up and learning how to be a man. I can therefore understand and accept why he found it impossible to forgive his father for leaving him. He would probably never have been able to come to terms with the fact that this might have been John's only way to secure a bearable future away from the dreadful guilt and haunting dreams of his lost sons.

The following words which conclude this book are Keturah's. She wrote them at the end of her memoirs as she paid her final tribute to her parents and reflected on what life had and still had to offer her.

I feel I must conclude on a personal note. Firstly I give thanks to my wonderful father for preparing us for the world outside as it was then, for his kind but strict discipline and for passing on his knowledge of the world that he had gained whilst sailing round the world. I thank my mother for her love, patience and strength which she bestowed on us. God bless her. Dearest Mum, how we loved her. I talk to her photograph to this day, and I am eighty two years old. I talk to my dad too, both were wonderful. If I could chose between the times in which I grew up and the present time I would choose the present generation. Now there is so much to learn and to do, with countless challenges awaiting young people if they will only reach out and grasp them. Don't waste those golden opportunities. My advice is, 'work hard and play hard' and then pass on what you have learnt to your own children, and so on and so on.

Bibliography

Filmer. Seven Generations of a Kent Family
John L Filmer 1975 The Research Publishing Company

The Leysdown Tragedy
Rex Batten 1992 Friends of Nunhead Cemetery

Sea Scouting. A History 1909-2009
Roy Masini 2009 amazon.co.uk

The Death of a Child
Edited by Peter Stanford 2011 Continuum International
Publishing Group

Life and Times at East Sutton Park, Rita Greenfield

A Family History, Rosemary Moore

Internet information:

'The decline of Infant Mortality and Fertility. Evidence from
British cities in demographic transition'. University of Sussex
Department of History 48-2012